FRUITS OF PARADISE

Fruits of Paradise

A Vegetarian Year-Book

❧

Rebecca Hall

SIMON & SCHUSTER

LONDON·SYDNEY·NEW YORK·TOKYO·SINGAPORE·TORONTO

First published in Great Britain by Simon & Schuster Ltd, 1993
A Paramount Communications Company

Simon & Schuster Ltd
West Garden Place
Kendal Street
London W2 2AQ

Simon & Schuster of Australia Pty Ltd
Sydney

A CIP catalogue record for this book is available from the British Library

ISBN 0-671-71323-X

Front cover illustration:
by Frank Brangwyn (1887–1956)
One of 18 panels now in the Brangwyn Hall, Swansea.
Originally commissioned for the House of Lords as a
memorial of the First World War, they were considered
too exuberant for that setting.
Brangwyn believed that the millions who died would
have wished to be remembered not by gory battle scenes
but by the joy and unison of life.

Designed & typeset in 10.5pt Galliard
at Five Seasons Press, Hereford
Printed & bound in Great Britain
by Butler & Tanner Ltd, Frome and London
on Five Seasons one hundred per cent recycled book paper

This book is dedicated to "I"
the True Inspiration

Many thanks are due to all who have so freely agreed to their contributions being used in this book, whose thoughts, words, ideals and vision, together with those who speak from times and ages past, have kept alive the hope for the compassionate way and are helping to create an atmosphere in which it may grow, prosper and flourish today.

The words collected here and arranged for reading through the year, for browsing, or as a work of reference are presented in a way which attempts to lead the thoughts from one piece to the next so as to inspire and expand the awareness. Bare facts may be followed by some exalted idea or small illustrative story which reveals something of the character of creatures. The pieces are drawn from many cultures and many times and will, I hope, show that humankind in its secret heart truly desires to live in The Peaceable Kingdom where none shall hurt nor destroy.

Prologue

What mocking elf, on impish mischief bent,
Called man, this barbarous Man, the sapient;

Yet nearer than he knew that jester came
To give rapacious Man the fitting name;
For change one single letter and behold -
In 'Homo Rapiens' the true tale is told.

AUTHOR UNKNOWN

They are slaves who fear to speak
For the fallen and the weak;
They are slaves who will not choose
Hatred, scoffing, and abuse,
Rather than in silence shrink,
From the truths they needs must think.
They are slaves who dare not be
In the right with two or three.

J R LOWELL 1819–1891

We who are deaf to suffering creatures' cries,
Remember that their sound goes up to heaven;
Perchance a day may come when we shall crave
For mercy to be given.

AUTHOR UNKNOWN

January 1

When man follows religious feeling or motion of the Divine Spirit within him, his vision is full of the Light of Life. And in that Light he sees and understands the manifestations of the Divine Mystery around him.

And he also comes to understand the spiritual nature of all things, and his own true relation to them. The wealth of the edible and esculent products within the realm of the vegetable kingdom, he recognizes as the glorious revelation of the Divine Provision for Humanity's needs, the illimitable enrichments given to the race by the Divine Love and Wisdom.

REV JOHN TODD FERRIER 1855–1943
On Behalf of the Creatures
The Order of the Cross 1926

January 2

No streams of blood are among them; no butchering and cutting up of flesh; no dainty cookery; no heaviness of head. Nor are there horrible smells of flesh-meats among them, or disagreeable fumes from the kitchen. No tumult or disturbance or wearisome clamours, but bread and water . . . If, however they may desire to feast more sumptuously, the sumptuousness consists in fruits, and their pleasure in these is greater than at royal tables.

JOHN CHRYSOSTOM C. 345–407
One of the fathers of the Greek Church, Archbishop of Constantinople
Homily LXXIX, chapter 3, (on St Matt., XXII, 1–14)
Close of chapter 4 speaking of those who had consecrated themselves to the highest ideals

January 3

And now a third, a Brazen people rise,
Unlike the former, men of monstruous size.

On the crude flesh of beasts, they feed alone,
Savage their nature, and their hearts of stone.

HESIOD 8th Century BC
Works and Days Book I Lines 191-201
Hesiod writing on the Three Ages of Man: the Golden, the Silver and the Brazen
Age. Hesiod belonged to the Orphic Society—supposed to have been founded by
Orpheus—who was said by Horatius to have introduced the reformation of diet
among his countrymen

≈ ≈

January 4

Greece and Rome in the height of their glory were practically
frugivorous . . . the decline and fall of Greece and Rome may be traced
back to the gross life that grew up as the result of voluptuous living.

REV J TODD FERRIER 1855–1943
On Behalf of the Creatures
The Order of the Cross 1926

January 5

But Buddha softly said:
'Let him not strike, great King!' and therewith loosed
The victim's bonds, none staying him, so great
His presence was. Then, craving leave he spake
Of Life which all can take but none can give.
Life which all creatures love and strive to keep,
Wonderful, dear, and pleasant unto each,
Given to the meanest: yea, a boon to all
Where pity is; for pity makes the world
Soft to the weak and noble for the strong—
Unto the dumb lips of his flock he lent
Sad, pleading words, showing how man, who prays
For mercy to the Gods, is merciless.
Being as God to these: albeit all life
Is linked and kin; and what we slay have
Meek tribute of the milk and wool given, and set
Fast trust upon the hands that murder them.
While still our Lord went on, teaching how fair
This earth were, if all living things be linked
In friendliness and common use of foods,
Bloodless and pure—the golden grain, bright fruits,
Sweet herbs, which grow for all, the waters wan,
Sufficient drinks and meats—which when these heard,
The might of gentleness so conquered them,
The priests themselves scattered their altar-flames
And flung away the steel of sacrifice;
And through the land next day passed a decree
Proclaimed by criers, and in this wise graved
On rock and column. Thus the King's will is:
'There hath been slaughter for the sacrifice,
And slaying for the meat, but henceforth none
Shall spill the blood of life, nor taste of flesh:
Seeing that knowledge grows, and life is one,
And mercy cometh to the merciful.'

SIR EDWIN ARNOLD (1832–1904)
English poet and traveller; translator of Indian, Persian and Turkish
The Light of Asia Book V, Lines 398-454

January 6

We follow the ways of wolves, the habits of tigers: or, rather we are worse than they. To them nature has assigned that they should be thus fed, while God has honoured us with rational speech and a sense of equity. And yet we are become worse than the wild beast.

JOHN CHRYSOSTOM, C. 345-407
Homily LXIX Chapter 4

January 7

I think that possibly you may like to reproduce an article which has recently appeared in a French newspaper, and of which, therefore, I enclose a translation. I have seen several of the advertisements, 'Bains de Sang' (Baths of Blood), to which the article refers, and I know a Parisian lady whose doctor told her that she would probably die if she did not consent to go to the slaughterhouse in the morning and drink blood. He said she had tubercular symptoms and that nothing else could save her. She refused to comply and recovered.

This 'blood mania' is, in fact, the last new medical craze, and it may interest your readers to see what is thus the practical outcome of vivisection and carnivorous tastes, encouraged as they are in this aesthetic city of Paris.

ANNA KINGSFORD MD 1846–1888.
Britain's first woman physician (qualified in Paris); mystic and seer, writer, campaigner for vegetarianism and against vivisection
Letter 1883

January 8

He who kills, kills himself; and whoso eats the flesh of slain beasts, eats of the body of death. For in his body every drop of their blood turns to poison, and their death will become his death.

He also said, I am come to end the sacrifices and feasts of blood, and if ye cease not offering and eating of flesh and blood, the wrath of God shall not cease from you, even as it came to your fathers in the wilderness, who lusted for flesh, and they did eat to their content, and were filled with rottenness, and the plague consumed them.

As you do in this life to your fellow creatures, so shall it be done to you in the life to come.

The Gospel of the Holy Twelve 1905
Translated from the original Aramaic and edited by a disciple of the Master, being one of the most ancient and complete of early Christian fragments
Received by Rev Gideon Jasper Richard Ouseley 1835–1906
Christian Gospel Trust

January 9

Of a certainty the man who can see all creatures in himself, himself in all creatures, knows no sorrow.

EESHA
Upanishad 10th Century BC
Part of Vedic literature: Sanskrit metaphysical treatises
Part of Hindu religion

January 10

Whatever treatment we give to lesser creatures is a reflection on the state of our soul in relation to their Creator.

CARDINAL RAFAEL SANTOS Archbishop of Manila
Pastoral letter, October 1963

January 11

Be kind to all that lives. He who does not injure any creature, obtains what he thinks of, what he undertakes and what he fixes his mind on.

THE BUDDHA (SIDDHARTHA GAUTAMA or SHAKYAMUNI)
c. 6TH CENTURY BC.

January 12

No human being, past the thoughtless age of boyhood, will wantonly murder any creature which holds its life by the same tenure that he does.

It may be vain to ask why the imagination will not be reconciled to flesh and fat. I am satisfied that it is not. Is it not a reproach that man is a carnivorous animal?

Man conceitedly names the intelligence and industry of animals instinct, and overlooks their wisdom and fitness of behaviour.

HENRY DAVID THOREAU 1817–1862
American essayist, naturalist and poet

January 13

The Essex Quaker Benjamin Hay, who emigrated to Philadelphia in 1731 had so tender a conscience that he would eat no food nor wear any garment which had been procured at the expense of animal life (or indeed at the cost of slave labour).

KEITH THOMAS
Man and the Natural World—Changing Attitudes in England 1500–1800

January 14

I think I could turn and live with animals, they are
      so placid and self-contained,
I stand and look at them long and long.

WALT WHITMAN 1819–1892
American poet, journalist and essayist
Leaves of Grass: 'Song of Myself'

January 15

They took him up into a mountain, but the beasts of the forest gathered round him like lambs.
   He was exposed in the amphitheatre but a lion and lioness let loose upon him only licked his hand and his feet.

SAINT ELEUTHERIUS.
Lives of Saints. II. 120

January 16

Every minute of each working day 3,000 animals are killed for food in the United Kingdom. 450,000,000 animals a year. Each day in the United States 9,000,000 chickens, turkeys, pigs, calves and cows are slaughtered for human consumption.   (1991)

January 17

As a priest of the worldwide Anglican communion I openly accuse each one of its branches of falsely portraying the love, mercy and compassion of God by making them far too small . . . to the leaders of each major denomination I would equally say: 'You take the God of the Bible and by your theology you shrink Him and His love as only embracing humanity! My God is concerned about the beasts of the field and the birds of the air (Psalm 50:10–11), whereas you have limited His love and all embracing compassion to your own motley species . . . So lacking in vital moral issues has Christendom become that it's not been unknown to tuck into veal at a religious retreat, or crack open battery eggs; while during the meal, a monk, nun or spiritual director reads an extract from some devotional work, if not the Bible itself—exemplifying the life of 'holiness'. . Let me tell you of a convent in Davenport where up to a few months ago, despite repeated protests by reputable animal rightists the nuns—who were encircled by acres of open land—when not engaged in regular prayer and worship, ran a highly lucrative 'battery farm' . . . where hens were over crammed in filthy cages and deprived of all exercise. Thankfully, due to constant protests from, it might appear, all but the 'religious!', their vile trade has now terminated. As . . . has the appalling veal farm of the monks at Storrington Priory . . .

One senses that if the scribes and pharisees picked out (moral) gnats while swallowing camels, then they didn't do it half as well as many so-called Christian leaders do it today. But then, perhaps it's expecting too much to assume that a humanely prepared dish akin to vegetarianism would be acceptable to those who live in palaces—and that's where leading prelates often live! . . . there certainly are things which are considered sinful which . . . religious communities will speak up about: the four lettered word; non attendance at mass; the taking of a pill or wearing of a Durex . . . . And all these things may well be discussed with much heated emotion. Yes, after one has indulged in, and enjoyed without a qualm of conscience, the products of animal Belsens!

REV JAMES THOMPSON 1930–
The Animals' Padre
'Retreat' From Responsibility. Christian Apathy and the Animal Cause.
St. Clement's Publications, Buckie, Scotland

January 18

If men were not so blind, so full of vain conceit, they would recognize the fact, attested by science and the sacred records, that in the scale of evolution man came last, that ere he appeared the various animals had uses all their own. Out of their own joy the birds sing, the cattle low, and all nature takes part in the universal harmony. So the animals were made for themselves, for their own joy, to fulfil some worthier function in nature than provide sumptuous repasts for men and women who have reversed the order of nature in themselves, and grown into carnivorous animals.

REV JOHN TODD FERRIER 1855–1943
On Behalf of the Creatures 1926
The Order of the Cross

January 19

Even if the scientific facts didn't tally, there are compelling spiritual reasons for vegetarianism. Consider, for instance, that the word 'spiritual' comes from the Latin *spiritus*, meaning 'breath', 'vigor', or 'life'. The word vegetarianism comes from the Greek *vegetas*, or 'full of the breath of life'. Even the etymology of the two words affirms their interrelation.

STEVEN ROSEN 1955–
Devout vegetarian; Vaishnava scholar, American writer and journalist
Food For The Spirit
Bala Books NY USA 1987

January 20

God endowed animals with a sense of joy in life according to their nature.

FATHER SCAVINI
Italian theologian

January 21

Nothing is foreign—parts relate to whole:
One all-extending, all-preserving soul
Connects each being, greatest with the least—
Made beast in aid of man, and man of beast;
   All served, all-serving—nothing stands alone.
Has God thou fool, worked solely for thy good,
Thy joy, thy pastime, thy attire, thy food?

ALEXANDER POPE 1688–1744
English neoclassical poet and satirist, literary dictator of his age
Essay on Man (III)

January 22

'Life', as Huxley stated in his introduction to the classification of Animals, 'is the course and not the consequence of organization.' In other words life can only be conceived as indissolubly connected with spirit and thought, and with the course of the directive energy everywhere manifested in the growth of living things. Its origin is unknown to science.

STANLEY DE BRATH CE 1854–1937
Government engineer (India), headmaster (England), noted English psychical researcher
The Functions of Life
London Spiritualist Alliance (now College of Psychic Studies) London 1937

January 23

Ask the very beasts and they will teach you
For which of them knows not that this is the Eternal's way.

JOB
The Old Testament of The Bible

January 24

Life's experiences carry us through a hundred forms; for it is thus we gain our manifoldness. Our evolution is through the various animal forms till our life is crowned with the angel. But where men and women strangle the angelic-aspiring life, they fashion to themselves new animal forms, it may be a lower human, or non-human.

We are what we think; as we desire so do we become! By our thoughts, desires and habits, we either ascend to the full divine dignity of our nature, or we descend to suffer and learn . . .

Though all sacred records said not one word in favour of a non-flesh diet, yet should the humane question command our sympathy, for the Law of God engraved on the altar of a humane soul aspiring to the Divine, is of more value than that written in a book.

And though history failed to support my contention, yet for humane reasons we should abstain, because in our life we are writing that history which is for us the most important in the world. And though science had not come to our aid to show the value of fruitarian diet in the body, yet the claims of the sentient creatures who are to shelter beneath the wing of our sympathy should constrain us to cease living upon their flesh. And though the new regimen of diet failed in its economic promise, yet kindness should ever sway us in our attitude to these non-human souls, as well as to men. For above all things the Divine Man is humane towards all life, and the inhumane man is not on the high road to divinity . . . and since we cannot be truly humane and yet kill the objects of our compassion in order to gratify our eating lusts, there is no other way left open for us, but the narrow way of righteous dealing towards the sub-human as towards the human.

REV JOHN TODD FERRIER 1855–1943
On Behalf of the Creatures 1926
The Order of The Cross

January 25

God is in every creature, so how can you give such pain?

SATYA SAI BABA 1926–
Indian Purna Avatara

January 26

Vegans seem . . . to have said, 'things are what they are; they will only get better if I change.' Instead of being discouraged by the enormity of ills besetting the world, they start by lessening the animal suffering, and healing seems to spread in a rippling effect.

VICTORIA MORAN 1950–
Compassion: The Ultimate Ethic
Thorsons 1985

January 27

The philosophy of non-violence which I learned from Dr Martin Luther King Jr during my involvement in the Civil Rights Movement was first responsible for my change in diet.

. . . Under the leadership of Dr King, I became totally committed to non-violence, and I was convinced that non-violence meant opposition to killing in any form. I felt the commandment 'Thou shalt not kill' applied to human beings not only in their dealings with each other—war, lynching, assassination, murder and the like—but in their practice of killing animals for food or sport. Animals suffer and die alike. Violence causes the same pain . . . the same arrogant, cruel and brutal taking of life.

One night . . . I made the decision never to eat meat again. I had become firmly convinced that the killing of animals for food was both immoral and unnatural.

DICK GREGORY
Comedian and crusader who turned vegetarian in 1965
Natural Diet for Folks Who Eat: Cooking With Mother Nature
Perennial Library New York 1974

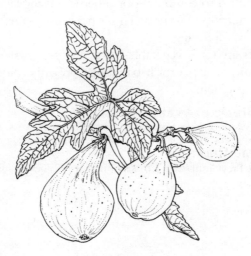

January 28

To avoid causing terror to living beings, let the Disciple refrain from eating meat . . . There may be some foolish people in the future who will say that I permitted meat-eating and that I partook of meat myself, but . . . meat-eating in any form, in any manner, and in any place, is unconditionally prohibited for all.

THE BUDDHA, (SIDDHARTHA GAUTAMA or SHAKYAMUNI)
c. 6th Century BC
The Lankavatara Sutra

January 29

We often hear meat spoken of as some sort of 'ideal' nutritional source that other kinds of foods must be measured by. Vegetable proteins are often spoken of as 'possibly adequate'—if a great deal of thought and effort is applied to combining or otherwise using them to make them 'almost as' nutritious as meat. This is nonsense—a result of many years of cultural conditioning.

The facts are (1) A vegetable-based diet presents virtually no nutritional problems, (2) A meat-based diet presents complex, even grave, nutritional problems.

JOHN A SCHARFFENBERG MD MPH
Adjunct Professor of Nutrition, Loma Linda University USA, and Vice-President, Pacific Health Education Centre, Bakersfield, California
Problems with Meat
Woodbridge Press Publishing Co. Santa Barbara, California 1989

January 30

To my mind the life of a lamb is no less precious than that of a human being. I should be unwilling to take the life of a lamb for the sake of a human body. I hold that, the more helpless a creature, the more entitled it is to protection by man, from the cruelty of man.

MOHANDAS KARAMCHAND GANDHI 1869–1948
Hindu leader of India's movement for independence
An Autobiography, the Story of my Experiments

January 31

Our little lamb He lent awhile
Pure as himself from stain:
Then said *my kingdom is of such*,
And called it home again.

F T PALGRAVE 1824–1897
English poet and critic

February 1

There can be no purity whilst the flesh of creatures is partaken of and inhumanity towards the creatures is practised. It is the accomplishment by the potencies of the Heavens of that redemptive state in which all the creatures are to share; for when the Redemption of man is fully realized, the conditions of life will all be changed. The prophetic visions will have found fulfilment, and the Soul's dream will have grown into a blessed realization. No more shall evil blight the life, nor sin come nigh the Soul's dwelling-place; for throughout the land there shall be the goodness of love, and in the kingdoms of the world peace shall reign. And thus shall the world's great hope come into fruition, man be at last crowned with the glory of perfected life, and the whole world be once more the scene of the most beautiful and blessed ministry unto all Souls and all creatures.

To such a glorious consummation does the inner meaning of the Food Reform Movement point the way.

REV JOHN TODD FERRIER 1855–1943
Herald Vol VII (p160)
The Order of The Cross 1911

February 2

He that killeth an ox is as he that slayeth a man; he that sacrificeth a lamb as he that breaketh a dog's neck.

ISIAH LXVI, 3

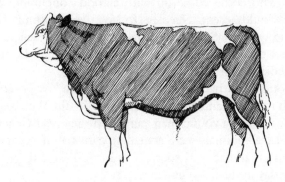

The wolf shall dwell with the lamb, and the leopard shall lie down with the kid and the calf and the young lion and the fatling together; and a little child shall lead them.

ISIAH XI, 6-8

February 3

Back in the 1940s, a lioness called Little Tyke made the news for her refusal to eat flesh . . . An extraordinarily gentle animal, she lived peacefully at Hidden Valley Ranch with many herbivores, some of whom, like the lamb named Becky, were her special friends . . . She was exceptionally healthy . . . One of the country's most skilled zoo curators pronounced her 'the best of her species' he had ever seen. But scientists repeatedly told Tyke's 'parents', Georges and Margaret Westbeau, that it was not possible for a lion to survive without eating flesh.

Concern for their beloved pet prompted them to offer $1,000 in cash to anyone who could come up with a food containing flesh which little Tyke would accept. Needless to say, many formulas were tried, but nothing worked. She could usually detect its presence, and would simply reject the food. If it was so well disguised that she ate the stuff, she'd immediately throw it up.

So, although they had worked out a diet Tyke loved—cooked grain mixed with raw milk and eggs from the ranch—the Westbeaus worried about her . . . until a young man suggested they read Genesis 1:30 . . . Reading that all animals were actually meant to eat vegetarian finally put their minds at ease . . . Especially as Little Tyke did spend about an hour every day in the fields grazing.

. . . Thousands upon thousands of Americans responded to the idea of a vegetarian lion with enthusiasm; some even shed tears of joy . . . The letters which swamped the Westbeaus after her TV appearance plainly illustrated that the dream of peace among all creatures is cherished in people's hearts.

BARBARA LYNN PETERS
American singer
Dogs and Cats Go Vegetarian
Harbingers of a New Age USA 1988

February 4

Vegetarianism is not a fad. It is a great and essential part of the religion of humanity. It is a step into a higher, because a less selfish plane of life. It makes progress possible, and both individual and social development is at present seriously blocked by the meat habit and all that it implies and involves.

As long as we treat other living, sensitive creatures with like feelings as ours only as carcasses for the market and meat to be consumed, we must shut our eyes to the real kinship of all living things, and thus lose an essential factor in learning to understand, even in some degree, this mysterious world in which we find ourselves. Social progress is blocked, no less than individual development. In a dozen ways this barbarous habit, inherited from savage ancestors, stands in the way of practical reforms which are much needed.

ERNEST BELL 1851–1933

February 5

Truly man is the king of beasts, for his brutality exceeds them. We live by the death of others. We are burial places! I have from an early age abjured the use of meat, and the time will come when men such as I will look upon the murder of animals as they now look upon the murder of men.

LEONARDO DA VINCI 1452–1519
Italian painter, sculptor, architect, engineer, scientist, poet and musician
Notes

February 6

The eating of meat extinguishes the seed of great compassion.

MAHAPAVINIRVANA

February 7

Not to hurt our humble brethren is our first duty to them, but to stop there is a complete misapprehension of the intentions of Providence. We have a higher mission—to be of service to them, whenever they require it.

FRANCIS OF ASSISI 1181–1226
Italian friar. Known especially for his simplicity, and a lyricism which manifested in his life. Friend and brother of all living things.
Life of St Francis by St Bonaventura

February 8

He who abstains from anything animate . . . will be much more careful not to injure those of his own species. For he who loves the genus will not hate any species of animals . . .

But to deliver animals to be slaughtered and cooked, and thus be filled with murder, not for the sake of nutriment and satisfying the wants of nature, but making pleasure and gluttony the end of such conduct, is transcendently iniquitous and dire.

PORPHYRY 233-304
Greek Neoplatonist. Student and biographer of Plotinus and a biographer of Pythagoras.
On Abstinence from Animal Food
Centaur Press 1965

February 9

'He looked like a butcher.'
The worst insult I can give to anyone is to say he looks like a butcher.

MAHATMA GANDHI 1869–1948
(Describing Benito Mussolini)

February 10

The wise look with an equal eye on a Brahmin, endowed with knowledge and humility, an untouchable, a cow, an elephant and a dog.

The Bhagavad Gita
An 18-part discussion between Krishna and Arjuna on the nature
and meaning of life   (Sanskrit: *The Song of God*)
Part of the *Mahabharata*   (Hindu scripture)

February 11

Some animals are much more sensitively organized than many people
are, and consequently they get the effect of our thoughts, our mental
states, and emotions much more readily than many people do. Therefore whenever we meet an animal we can do it good by sending out
to it these thoughts of love. It will feel the effects whether we simply
entertain or whether we voice them. And it is often interesting to
note how quickly it responds, and how readily it gives evidence of its
appreciation of this love and consideration on our part.

RALPH WALDO TRINE   1866–1958
American writer
In Tune with the Infinite (1897)
Reprinted by Collier Books (Macmillan) 1986

February 12

A lamb had been sent to be killed. While waiting its turn it came out of the pen, came up to the slaughterers, who were getting a meal, evidently to be petted, it ate pieces of bread from their hands and they all played with it. When killing time came they individually declined to do the job, and it had to be sent back to the farm from which it came.

The Meat Trades Journal Sept 7th 1939

February 13

I first heard of the theory that crime and violence proliferate near slaughterhouses from my brother when he returned from a few years living in the USA. My nearest town is Chard, in Somerset. It is only a small town, a population of less than 10,000, and has no great historical claims to fame—in fact, all in all it seems pretty insignificant. However, it so happens that Chard contains one of the biggest, if not *the* biggest, slaughterhouse in the entire European Economic Community. To my amazement, when I enquired at the local police station about Chard's crime rate, a slightly embarrassed policeman informed me that Chard's crime rate per head of population was second only to Glasgow!

JOHN BRYANT 1942–
Former manager of Ferne Animal Sanctuary; former chairman of Animal Aid; head of press and research for the League Against Cruel Sports
Fettered Kingdoms
(The slaughterhouse has since closed and a new food wholesale company has been built on the site, managed by a vegetarian)

February 14

When anyone eats the flesh of the creatures he takes into himself all the influences of the creature who functioned through the body from which it was taken. These influences do not pass out of his body, but are absorbed by it, and so the flesh eaten is constantly storing up these evil emanations. This means that, in addition to his own animal nature, he has these other animal conditions to overcome. But the result is that they gradually overcome him, in the sense that his animal nature becomes so strong that it becomes more and more difficult for the soul to function truly. In the end many of our fellow men function exclusively on the intellectual or even on the merely physical plane, and they are quite unable to perceive the things of the spirit. This explains why so many people are quite unable to understand anything beyond the outward and literal meaning of spiritual things. And it is also the reason for the obvious inconsistency of religious people.

REV V A HOLMES-GORE
These We Have Not Loved
C W Daniel Co Ltd, 1942

February 15

It may startle you to know that next to tobacco and alcohol, the use of meat is probably the greatest single cause of mortality in the United States. This is likely also the case in some other 'affluent' societies.

It may also startle you to know that, contrary to common opinion, it is *more difficult* to have a good diet *with* meat than without it—and that you don't have to worry about complicated 'protein supplementation' to have ample proteins in both quality and quantity, in a simple vegetarian diet.

JOHN A SCHARFFENBERG MD
Problems With Meat
Woodbridge Press California 1979 & 1989

February 16

It is a great delusion to suppose that flesh-meat of any kind is essential to health. Considerably more than three parts of the work of the world is done by men who never taste anything but vegetable, farinaceous food, and that of the simplest kind. There are far more strength-producing properties in wholemeal flour, peas, beans, lentils, oatmeal, roots, and other vegetables of the same class, than there are in beef or mutton, poultry or fish, or animal food of any description whatever.

Orders and Regulations of the Officers of the Salvation Army
Christian Evangelical, social service and social reform organization, originally British but later worldwide. Begun by William Booth in 1865 and named Salvation Army in 1878.

February 17

A meat and dairy diet requires much more land than a vegetarian or vegan diet would . . . An American type diet requires 0.62 hectares per head, while a vegan diet would only need 0.08 hectares per head. There is *more than enough* arable land per head to support the world's population, at the present level or at the foreseeable future level *on a vegan diet*, but *nowhere near enough land for the extravagant animal produce centred American one.*

GEOFFREY YATES 1904–1989
School teacher, vegetarian and ecologist
Food: Need, Greed & Myopia. Exploitation and Starvation in a World of Plenty.
Earthright Publications 1986

February 18

Alas, what wickedness to swallow flesh into our own flesh, to fatten our greedy bodies by cramming in other bodies, to have one living creature fed by the death of another! In the midst of such wealth as earth, the best of mothers, provides, nothing forsooth satisfies you, but to behave like the Cyclopes, inflicting sorry wounds with cruel teeth! You cannot appease the hungry cravings of your wicked, gluttonous stomachs by destroying some other life.

PYTHAGORAS 6th Century BC
Greek philosopher and mathematician
Depicted by Ovid in *The Metamorphoses* (translated by Mary M Innes)

February 19

A dinner!
How horrible!
I am to be made the pretext for killing all those wretched animals and birds, and fish!
Thank you for nothing.
Now if it were to be a fast instead of a feast; say, a solemn three day's abstention from corpses in my honour, I could at least pretend to believe that it was disinterested.
Blood sacrifices are not in my line.

GEORGE BERNARD SHAW 1856–1950
Irish dramatist, critic and social reformer
Letter 30.12.1929

February 20

'Thou shalt not kill,' does not apply to murder of one's own kind only, but to all living beings, and this Commandment was inscribed in the human breast long before it was proclaimed from Sinai.

LEO TOLSTOY 1828–1910
Russian novelist and moral philosopher, playwright and essayist

February 21

The crow and the sparrow are my kin,
The wide seas and hills are my clan.
Whatever I see, wherever my eyes turn,
I see my own flesh and blood,
I see myself in every being around,
Oh what boundless joy!

BHARATI
Tamil poet

February 22

Phythagoras, who believed in the transmigration of souls, taught kindness to animals, and is said on one occasion to have purchased from some fishermen all the fish in their net, that he might have the pleasure of setting them free.

REV V A HOLMES-GORE MA
These We Have Not Loved
C W Daniel 1942

February 23

The same Power formed the sparrow
That fashioned man—the king;
The God of the whole gave a living soul
To furred and feathered thing.
And I am my brother's keeper,
And I will fight his fight;
And speak the word for beast and bird
Till the world shall set things right.

ELLA WHEELER WILCOX 1850–1919
English poet

February 24

The birds of the aire die to sustain thee;
The beasts of the field die to nourish thee;
The fishes of the sea die to feed thee.
Our stomachs are their common sepulcher.
Good God! With how many deaths are our poor lives patcht up!
How full of death is the life of momentary man!

FRANCIS QUARLES 1592–1644
English metaphysical poet
Enchyridion

February 25

When first it dawned on human wisdom that the same thing breathed in animals as in mankind, it appeared too late to avert the curse which, ranging ourselves with the beasts of prey, we seemed to have called down upon us through the taste of animal food: disease and misery of every kind, to which we did not see vegetable-eating man exposed. The insight thus obtained led further to the consciousness of a deep-seated guilt in our earthly being; it moved those fully seized therewith to turn aside from all that stirs the passions, through total abstinence from animal food. To these wise men the mystery of the world unveiled itself as a restless tearing into pieces, to be restored to restful unity by nothing save compassion . . . But still more to be deplored that wise man deemed the human being who consciously could torture animals and turn a deaf ear to their pain, for he knew that such a one was infinitely farther from redemption than the wild beast itself, which should rank in comparison as sinless as a saint.

RICHARD WAGNER 1813–1883
German composer, conductor and author
Essay: *Religion and Art*

February 26

Fish have for far too long been excluded from the Animal Rights Movement. Only vegetarians and vegans have given them consideration. But they have not publicized their plight, they have merely refrained from eating them.

Our conscience has been suppressed completely as far as fishes are concerned. They are mercilessly taken from their natural environment, heaped up and subjected to slow death by the pressure of the heaps, gasping for breath. Live and half-live fishes are cut up for sale in many countries . . . Millions are caught every day . . . people have been so thoughtless, callous and heartless about fishes; they have no conscience about torturing and killing them. If we resort to cruelty and killing for food, we forsake morality.

SWAMI AVYAKTANANDA 1904–1990
Spiritual teacher and writer. Leader of the Vedanta Movement in Britain.
Vedanta Conference on Animal Liberation, Bath, August 1980
Vedanta: One of the leading systems of Hindu philosophy

February 27

Some say that He who gladly bore
His cross to Calvary and died
That men might of their earthly pride
Repent and enter Heaven's door,
Will to this wearied world once more,
Where war and greed and hate abide,
Return and pour a mighty tide
Of peace and love from shore to shore.

Master of masters, if Thou come
Be not for us alone Thy strife
But for the friendless and the dumb
Who share with us this gift of life.
Scourge from the temple of the soul
Those creeds of blood which still control.

ROBERT R LOGAN

∾ ∾

February 28

A cow lactates for ten months after producing a calf, but she comes back into heat three weeks after calving. On the next heat, six weeks after calving, she will be served once again by a bull, or she will be artificially inseminated. When her milk dries, it will only be six to eight weeks before she is calving again. If, because of her age, or for some other reason, she becomes barren, her productive life ends, yielding no monetary gain; her life will be taken from her. Barren cows eat, rather than produce profit and no farmer can, or will stand for that.

PETER ROBERTS 1924–
Former dairy farmer. Founder of Compassion in World Farming.
From an interview in *Voiceless Victims* by Rebecca Hall (Wildwood House 1984)

February 29

And Mount Sinai was altogether in smoke because the Lord descended upon it in fire: and the whole mount quaked greatly . . .

And the Lord called unto Moses out of the mountain, saying, 'Come unto me, for I would give thee the law for the Children of Light . . .

Thou shalt not take the life from any living thing. Life comes only from God, who giveth it and taketh it away.'

The Gospel of the Essenes
Translated from the original Hebrew & Aramaic texts by Edmund Bordeaux Szekely
C W Daniel 1976

❧ ❧

March 1

Cows

The cows graze in the field beside this house.
Gentle friends, I wish them the right to a natural death
In dignified old age.

Yesterday I saw a farmer who looked just like a cow,
But ugly for being human;
His poor, thick, red head stood out fatly,
His slow movements bespoke ponderous thoughts.

Later we talked of cow's heads offered by butchers:
I wonder if dogs would tear at his boiled head?
Or if fussy English people would relish
His nicely boiled and compressed pink tongue
Between slices of white bread
For tea on the lawn?
And if they did, would they know the difference?
And if they did, would they, finally, care?

REBECCA HALL
Writer
The Extended Circle—An Anthology of Humane Thought (Jon Wynne-Tyson)
Cardinal 1990

March 2

Whatever my own practice may be, I have no doubt that it is a part of the destiny of the human race, in its gradual improvement, to leave off eating animals, as surely as the savage tribes have left off eating each other when they came in contact with the more civilized.

HENRY DAVID THOREAU 1817–1862
Walden

☙ ☙

March 3

One reason why anyone who desires to develop his spirituality should, if his condition otherwise permit it, adopt a vegetarian diet, is that the flesh of animals exercises a stimulating effect upon the lower and animal instincts, which ought to be overcome instead of being aroused. The scientific explanation of this action of flesh is, that each material thing is one expression of its soul, and that it contains some of the qualities of that soul or life (karma), and communicates them to a certain extent to those in whom it is taken up.

BOMBASTUS PARACELSUS 1493–1541
Swiss physician and alchemist
From *The Life of Paracelsus* by Franz Hartmann

March 4

There is an essential and intimate connection between the carnivorous diet and the age of violence in which we live. This age of violence has continued for thousands of years, and nobody knows how much longer it will continue. We can only expect that, as the technique of violence becomes more scientific and wholesale, the story of man's degradation may soon end in the extermination of the human race and of all other life on earth.

But to accept this prospect would be to despair. We are bound to hope that it will be countered . . . The most radical means of curing man's addiction to violence would be the reform of his diet; and this is perhaps the only answer to the problem.

As things are in society, man is conditioned to violence and bloodshed from his earliest years by the uncivilized belief that it is necessary for him to kill and eat animals in order to live. Being firm in this belief, he (or she) can see nothing but fun in the cruel massacres perpetrated in the name of 'sport'.

For this it is but . . . an easy step to accepting the dismemberment and massacre of one's fellow men.

REV BASIL WRIGHTON 1900–1988
The Golden Age Must Return (A Catholic's View on Vegetarianism)
The British Vegetarian Nov/Dec 1965

March 5

And as Jesus was going to Jericho there met him a man with a cage full of birds which he had caught and some young doves. And he saw how they were in misery having lost their liberty, and moreover being tormented with hunger and thirst.

And he said to the man, 'What dost thou with these?' And the man answered, 'I go to make my living by selling these birds which I have taken.'

And Jesus said, 'What thinkest thou, if another, stronger than thou or with greater craft, were to catch thee and bind thee, or thy wife, or thy children, and cast thee into a prison, in order to sell thee into captivity for his own profit, and to make a living?

Are not these thy fellow creatures, only weaker than thou? And doth not the same God our Father-Mother care for them as for thee? Let these thy little brethren and sisters go forth into freedom, and see that thou do this thing no more, but provide honestly for thy living.'

And the man marvelled at these words and at his authority, and he let the birds go free. So when the birds came forth they flew unto Jesus and stood on his shoulder and sang unto him.

And the man inquired further of his doctrine, and he went his way, and learnt the craft of making baskets, and by this craft he earned his bread, and afterwards he broke his cages and his trays, and became a disciple of Jesus.

The Gospel of the Holy Twelve Ch 41 v 1-7
Received and translated by Rev G J R Ouseley, 1835–1906, being from an original Aramaic document

∽ ∾

March 6

St Anselm, as his life reveals, was moved to feelings of compassion for animals, and he wept for them when he saw them caught in the hunter's net.

ST ANSELM OF CANTERBURY 1033–1109
Recorded by Cornelus à Lapide. Bishop and theologian
(In the *Paradiso* (Canto xii) Dante mentioned St Anselm among the spirits of light and power in the Sphere of the Sun)

March 7

The Rev Gideon Jasper Ouseley was born in Lisbon on 15 October 1835 . . . and was educated at Dublin University.

He was ordained as a clergyman of the Established Church . . . and was appointed Curate of Warrenpoint Co Down in 1861.

But he did not long remain in a Church in which he found himself to be in a false position; and in 1870, having voluntarily renounced all eating of flesh, strong drink and tobacco, as inconsistent with the humanity and the true religion of Christ, as taught by Him and His apostles, he was received as a priest of the Catholic Apostolic Church.

. . . While he was not a sectarian and hated to be dubbed as such, he would work with all true reformers and good men who would try to bring people into ways of righteousness and raise them out of their barbarous habits of flesh-eating, strong drinking, and cruelty of any sort and kind.

He considered that 'the direct cause of poverty, bad health and social misery was due to flesh-eating, alcoholic drinking and tobacco smoking.' He saw in their abolition 'the only effectual means of the world's redemption, whether as regards men themselves or the animals.' 'The true and proper food for man was that which Mother Earth brought forth in plenty for the sustenance of her children.'

. . . The Gospel of the Holy Twelve was received by the Rev Ouseley 'in dreams and visions of the night', and in 'communications'. It was a translation of an original Aramaic document purporting to be a reconstruction and revision of the Gospel narrative.

In Memoriam: The Gospel of the Holy Twelve

March 8

What right do we have to take away a life—human or non-human? To believe that the life of a cow or a snake is not important in this very intricate and complicated balance of nature is to deny the fundamental principle of ecology that every living thing is inextricably linked to each other.

We humans have unfortunately assumed ourselves to be the Lord of the universe and therefore, can do whatever we like with impunity, whereas science tells us that man is just a tiny dot in a big circle representing the universe . . .

Our next evolutionary stage must be, for our own sake, where we extend the definition of cannabalism to include eating of non-human animals . . . as an eminent scientist J B S Haldane put it, 'the distinction between eating goats and cannibalism appears rather thin,' and 'my claim to a more immortal soul than a goat is not strong enough to justify me in eating the goat.' The Commandment, 'Thou shalt not kill', which has no exceptions and no ifs and no buts for any form of life, 'must be binding on the conscience of humanity.'

SURINDER NATH GUPTA MA 1933–
Indian teacher, writer and vegetarian living in Canada
Vegetarianism: A Human Imperative
Bharatiya Vidya Bharan, Bombay 1986

☙ ❧

March 9

I suggest that in proportion as man is truly 'humanized', not by schools of cookery but by schools of thought, he will abandon the barbarous habit of his flesh-eating ancestors, and will make gradual progress towards a purer, simpler, more humane, and therefore more civilized diet-system.

HENRY SALT 1831–1939
English writer, critic, essayist, poet and humanitarian reformer
The Humanities of Diet

48

March 10

While we ourselves are the living graves of murdered beasts, how can we expect any ideal conditions on this earth?

GEORGE BERNARD SHAW 1856–1950

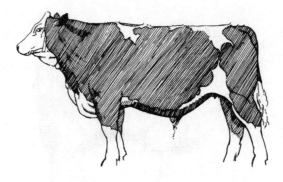

March 11

I'm sorry I got so mad at you before. It's not your fault. You are just showing me what I already know, but try not to think about. It just tears me up, some of the things we are doing to these animals. These pigs never hurt anybody, but we treat them like, like, like I don't know what. Nothing in the world deserves this kind of treatment. It's a shame. It's a crying shame. I just don't know what else to do.

A pig farmer to John Robbins
(John Robbins: heir to Baskin-Robbins, the world's largest ice-cream company, which he repudiated. Author, President of Earth Save Foundation.)
Diet For A New America
Stillpoint 1987

March 12

Man has an infinite capacity to rationalize his rapacity, especially when it comes to something he wants to eat.

CLEVELAND AMORY
American journalist, writer and animal rights campaigner
Founder-president of the Fund For Animals, New York

March 13

Ritual slaughter was first. The sheep are brought in one at a time (or three at a time, if nobody's looking) and placed, back down, on a low table. Their throats are then sliced with a sharp knife whilst their back leg is being shackled; then up the hoist to bleed to death. This, of course, is assuming that the first cut works. Otherwise the slaughterman finds himself with a fight on his hands as the sheep rolls around the floor in agony of its own blood. These sheep are 'awkward buggers' or 'stupid bastards' because they don't want to be killed.

KATHRYN REYNOLDS
Watching the Blood Run Cold
Outrage   (Animal Aid Sep/Oct 1983)

March 14

I laugh when I hear folks talk hopefully of the coming age, which will decide all the quarrels of the world by means of international arbitration and I have myself been scores of times invited to take part in 'Women's Peace Conventions' and the like. These poor deluded creatures cannot see that universal peace is absolutely impossible to a carnivorous race! If men feed like lions and tigers, they will, by the necessity of things, retain the nature of lions and tigers.

ANNA KINGSFORD MD   1846–1888
in a letter to her collaborator Edward Maitland
Quoted in Edward Maitland's *Life of Anna Kingsford*
George Redway London 1896

March 15

After World War II, scientists began for the first time to compile comprehensive statistics correlating the diet-styles and health of all the populations of the world.

One fact that emerged consistently was the strong correlation between heavy flesh-eating and short life expectancy. The Eskimos, Laplanders, the Greenlanders and the Russian Kurgi tribes stood out as the populations with the highest animal flesh consumption in the world—and also as among the populations with the lowest life expectancies, often only about 30 years.

It was found, further, that this was not due to the severity of their climates alone. Other peoples, living in harsh conditions, but subsisting with little or no animal flesh, had some of the highest life expectancies in the world. World health statistics found, for example, that an unusually large number of the Russian Caucasians, the Yucatan Indians, the East Indian Todas and the Pakistan Hunzakuts have life expectancies of 90–100 years.

JOHN ROBBINS
Diet For A New America
Stillpoint 1987

March 16

Man, carnivorous and sustaining himself by slaughter and torture, was not for her man at all in any true sense of the term. Neither intellectually nor physically could he be at his best while thus nourished.

The four points of her charter were: 'Purity of diet, compassion for the animals, the exaltation of womanhood, and mental and moral unfoldment through the purification of the organism.

EDWARD MAITLAND MA 1824–1907
(Writing about Anna Kingsford)

March 17

Life is life's greatest gift. Guard the life of another creature as you would your own because it *is* your own. On life's scale of values, the smallest is no less precious to the creature who owns it than the largest . . .

LLOYD BIGGLE JR
The Light That Never Was

March 18

Vegetable diet and sweet repose. Animal food and nightmare. Pluck your body from the orchard; do not snatch it from the shambles. Without flesh diet there could be no bloodshedding war.

LOUISA MAY ALCOTT 1832–1888
American novelist and poet
Life Letters & Journals

March 19

One man is proud when he has caught a poor hare, and another when he has taken a little fish in a net, and another when he has taken wild boars, and another when he has taken bears . . . Are not these robbers?

MARCUS AURELIUS (ANTONINUS) 121–180
Roman emperor and stoic philosopher
Meditations

March 20

Ahimsa—Non-violence (One of the four pillars of Jainism)
The universe is not for man alone, it is a field of evolution for all living beings. 'Live and let live' is the motto of Jainism. Life is sacred . . . to all living beings . . . right down to the tiny ant or the humble worm.

There is not an inch of space in the Universe where there are not innumerable, minute living beings . . .

A man cannot even sit quietly and breathe, without killing and harming life around him.

Then . . . How can a man live in this world without taking life and thereby committing violence? . . .

It demands constant vigilance. Where an action is performed with due care not to hurt anyone, no violence is committed. The emphasis is on the word "Care" . . .

Man in his desire to continue his life so that he may do the highest good while living here, is obliged to destroy life; but the fewer and the lower the forms of life he destroys, the less harmful *Karmas* or deeds he generates. This leads to strict vegetarianism . . .

The principle of *Ahimsa* has great potential significance because it is basic in concept and universal in its moral principles.

A great Jain scholar of the 10th Century, said, "In happiness or suffering, in joy or grief, we should regard all creatures as we regard our own self. We should therefore, refrain from inflicting upon others such injury as would appear undesirable to us, if inflicted upon ourselves."

POOJYA SHREE CHITRABANU
The first Jain master to leave India to travel to acquaint people with the principles of non-violence and the spiritual birthright of every individual
Sense Beyond the Senses
Jain Meditation International Centre, New York 1971

March *21*

We must be reminded that each morning as dawn breaks, millions upon millions of animals are slaughtered for food in town and village the world over: death on production lines, death en masse, industrial death; they see it, smell it, they know it is coming. Neither sight nor their instincts deceive them. They *know*. More horrible still is death by ritual slaughter, drawn out to last as long as the prayers said after them! What God could want that (for our survival . . .)?

We must be reminded what transportation means for them—by sea, by road or by train. Destined for the slaughterhouse, crammed together without food or water, they trample each other in the pounding vehicles or heaving seas. Hooves broken, eyes blinded, they die for lack of air, freeze to death or expire from heat. What does it matter . . .? They are to die in any case (for our survival . . .)?

BRIGITTE BARDOT 1934–
French filmstar and now famous for her animal rights work
From the foreword to *Voiceless Victims* (Rebecca Hall)
Wildwood House 1984

⮜ ⮞

March *22*

Creatures are ours to handle as we would touch the strings of a lyre, to intone a melodious song to God.

MARTINEZ
The Sanctifier

March 23

As the environment crisis heats up, it becomes obvious that the Age of Man the Exploiter is over. He is wasting his resources and fouling his nest. The Age of the New Man is dawning. He bases his life on reverence for all life. The vegan is the prototype of the New Man of the New Age.

KATHLEEN JANNAWAY 1915–
Secretary of the Vegan Society from 1971 to 1984;
joint co-ordinator of the Movement for Compassionate Living
The Vegan, Summer 1972

☙ ❧

March 24

Veganism is a way of living on the products of the plant kingdom to the exclusion of flesh, fish, fowl, eggs, animal milk and its derivatives (the taking of honey being left to individual conscience). It encourages the study and use of alternatives for all commodities normally derived wholly or partly from animals.

The objects of The Vegan Society are to further knowledge of, and interest in, sound nutrition and in the vegan method of agriculture and food production as a means of increasing the potential of the earth to the physical, moral and economic advantage of mankind.

Vegan Society—Policy Statement 1980

March 25

. . . Love and Unity are the foundations of our Creation . . . the eternal conquest of all wrong and suffering will be accomplished by means of gentleness and love . . . Nearly 2,500 years ago the Lord Buddha showed to the world the wrongness of sacrificing the lower creatures. Humanity already owes a mighty debt to the animals which it has tortured and destroyed, and far from any good resulting to man from such inhuman practices, nothing but harm and damage can be wrought to both the human and animal kingdoms. How far have we of the West wandered from those beautiful ideals of our Mother India of old times, when so great was the love for the creatures of the earth that men were trained and skilled to attend the maladies and injuries of not only the animals but also the birds. Moreover, there were vast sanctuaries for all types of life, and so averse were the people to hurting a lower creature that any man who hunted was refused the attendance of a physician in times of sickness until he had vowed to relinquish such a practice.

DR EDWARD BACH   1886–1936
Doctor of homoeopathy and healer;
discoverer of the Bach Flower system of healing
Heal Thyself
C W Daniel 1931

March 26

Doctors and scientists working with biogenic principles for restoring health and normal weight to their patients have long been aware that many of the reasons why living foods such as fresh raw fruits and vegetables and life-generating foods such as seeds or sprouts are so beneficial for reducing fat deposits can only begin to be explained fully once we have a better grasp of just how those subtle energies in biogenic and bioactive foods act upon our living systems to encourage detoxification, to heighten enzyme activity, to improve cellular metabolism, to encourage fat burning and to foster the quite marvellous kind of internal living sculpture which can restore some of the most neglected of overweight bodies to their natural lean forms.

LESLIE KENTON
British author and journalist;
former Health and Beauty Editor of *Harpers and Queen*
The Biogenic Diet
Arrow Books 1986

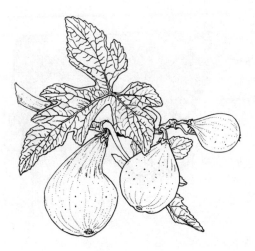

March 27

On the average, consumption of protein exceeds our needs by 66–75 per cent . . . The surplus protein is a source of energy. But amongst food-stuffs proteins are the least profitable energy-suppliers; they have slight 'use', their specific dynamic action overworks the regulators, and thus damages and undermines the whole organism. Meat is the principal culprit . . . the part assigned to protein in human food should amount to vegetable proportions only . . . As far back as Old Testament times (Book of Daniel) it was known that meat-eating is not good for health. Whenever in history wealth and luxury have spread, the consumption of meat increased. With it went disordered diet, and so—decline.

DR BIRCHER-BENNER 1867–1939
Swiss doctor and nutritionist who cured seemingly hopeless cases of disease with a raw vegetable diet; inventor of muesli
The Prevention of Incurable Disease
James Clarke 1981

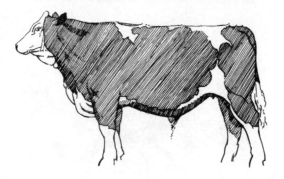

March 28

Meats of all kinds are unnatural foods. Flesh, fish, fowl and sea foods are very likely to contain numbers of germs. Meat contains bacteria. This bacteria infects the intestines causing colitis, and many other diseases. They always cause putrefaction.

   Research has shown beyond all doubt that a meat diet produces cancer in some cases. Excessive uric acid is caused by meat-eating. Excessive uric acid causes rheumatism, Bright's disease, kidneystones, gout, gallstones.

. . . Meat is an expensive second-hand food material and will not make healthy pure blood, or form good tissues.

JETHRO KLOSS 1863–1946
American herbalist, author, inventor, teacher and food scientist
Back to Eden
Back to Eden Books USA 1992

March 29

Our bodies are given to us to serve far higher purposes than we ordinarily use them for. In the degree that we come into the realization of the higher powers of the mind and spirit, in that degree does the body, through their influence upon it, become less gross and heavy, firmer in its texture and form. And then, because the mind finds a kingdom of enjoyment in itself, and in all the higher things it becomes related to, *excesses* in eating and drinking, as well as all others, naturally and of their own accord fall away. There also falls away the desire for the heavier, grosser, less valuable kinds of food and drink such as the flesh of animals, alcoholic drinks, and all things of the class that stimulate the body and the passions rather than build the body and brain into a strong, clean, well-nourished, enduring and fibrous condition. In the degree that the body thus becomes less gross and heavy, firmer in its texture and form, is there less waste, and what there is is more easily replaced, so that it keeps in a more regular and even condition.

As the body in this way grows firmer, in other words, as the process of its evolution is thus accelerated, it in turn helps the mind and the soul in the realization of even higher perceptions, and thus body helps mind just as mind builds body.

RALPH WALDO TRINE
In Tune With The Infinite
1897

March 30

This seems to be still the age of infancy, and baby-like do we cry 'This is all made by me!' The land and the ocean abound with myriads of animated beings of admirable construction only for me to play with, to torment, and to destroy. This is what we are taught . . .

Would that I could discover the affection of man for his relatives, to surpass that of brutes! . . . it is manifest that animals which are used for food seem to be aware of their danger . . . Who is ignorant that a sheep dreads a butcher's shop? . . .

Cruelty . . . always being the same, how terrible must be the result of encouraging it in any instance!

It is too evident that the passion for it being once excited, soon extends itself beyond the bounds prescribed, and objects of the brute creation alone do not satisfy its craving; human beings then become the sacrifice and tyranny and bloodshed the result.

LEWIS GOMPERTZ 1779–1861

Jewish advocate of rights for women, blacks, the poor, animals and all oppressed beings. A philosopher and inventor he would eat no animal products whatsoever, rejected the use of wool and silk and refused to ride in a horse-drawn carriage.
Moral Enquiries On The Situation of Man and of Brutes
Centaur Press 1992

March 31

And Jesus answered . . . But he who kills a beast without a cause, though the beast attack him not, through lust for slaughter, or for its flesh, or for its hide, or yet for its tusks, evil is the deed which he does, for he is turned into a wild beast himself. Wherefore is his end also as the end of the wild beasts.

The Gospel of Peace of Jesus Christ—The Disciple John
Translated from the original Aramaic texts by Edmund Szekely & Purcell Weaver
C W Daniel 1937

⟨. .⟩

April 1

Accumulated 'uric acid' heats up the blood to such an extent that the lower instincts (enemies) like lust, anger etc are much excited, furious quarrels and even the demoniac fears are also engendered by such hot blood. Modern research also endorses the view that fish, meat and eggs produce excess of 'uric acid' and for this reason, the Indian Masters have never accepted flesh foods as human diet. It is a diet of carnivorous animals . . .

Regular intake of flesh foods keeps the glands constantly over-active which leads to their depression and kidneys then fail to drain out the entire quantity of uric acid, the accumulation whereof causes depression of the glands and nerves of the whole body. Thus the body becomes vulnerable to any disease.

SWAMI SHIVANANDA SARASWATI 1890–1979
Innovator of a yogic system to cure mental and physical disease
Yogic Way To Cure Diseases
Umachal Yogashram, India 1957, 1978, 1985

April 2

. . . Recently the industrialization of the food industry has enabled animal foods, previously the privilege of only the rich, to be eaten daily by the average man, and so modern man has literally eaten his way back to the Ice Ages through the carcasses of beasts. As the cause of mental and physical sin, no wonder meat stands out with the redness of blood. Man pays for the sin of unnecessary slaughter by the slaughter of his own kind; the revenge for the horror of the slaughterhouse is the battlefield.

FRANK AVRAY WILSON 1914–
Nutritionist and Biologist
Food For The Golden Age
C W Daniel 1954

April 3

Ours is the world's most ferocious predatory species.

Exploitation of farm animals as little more than meat, milk and eggs on legs has intensified into the vicious rapine of factory farming. Bizarre environments, feeds, and boosters and manipulation of the animals' reproductive and maternal functions with a torrent of drugs masqueraded as 'animal health products' as surrogates for care, have loaded the markets with 'cheap' foods of animal origin costing dear in terms of callousness, waste, pollution and heavily-subsidized distortions of trade and distribution of resources.

Most of Britain's beef originates in the dairy herd. As much—or more—cruelty attends one pound of 'vegetarian' cheese as one pound of beef. BSE (mad cow disease) is just one of the evils overtaking the 'contented' cow, turned from gentle herbivorous archetype into carnivore and even cannibal and into a major agent of pollution.

Raw flesh, milk and eggs carry their contamination to other foods. Their dire effects are hardly surprising. They are produced in the conditions of an ill-kept lavatory.

We can live and let live in a green and pleasant land. Respect for it and all its denizens must oust industries devoted to breeding, rearing and killing animals in factories. Grow food, not feed must be the message for the world's agriculture.

ALAN LONG PHD 1925–
Organic chemist, biochemist, nutritionist; research advisor to VEGA (Vegetarian Economy and Green Agriculture)

April 4

This is dreadful! Not the suffering and death of the animals, but that man suppresses in himself, unnecessarily, the highest spiritual capacity—that of sympathy and pity towards living creatures like himself—and by violating his own feelings becomes cruel. And how deeply seated in the human heart is the injunction not to take life!

LEO TOLSTOY 1828–1910

April 5

I have had a lifelong inclination to eat the kind of food that our physiological structure shows we were intended to consume. Resistant from pramhood, as are most children, to meat and cow's milk, it took only the squeals of a pig being dragged to slaughter to set my infant teeth firmly on course for a fleshless future. My mother being half inclined that way herself, my urge was given its head instead of being hammered out of me, as it is out of so many young children who instinctively resist being made to eat substances their bodies were never designed to accept.

JON WYNNE-TYSON 1924–
British publisher and writer, concerned with animal rights and especially the adoption of the vegetarian/vegan diet
Food For A Future
Centaur Press 1979, Thorsons 1988

April 6

If true, the Pythagorean principles as to abstaining from flesh foster innocence; if ill-founded they at least teach us frugality, and what loss have you in losing your cruelty? I merely deprive you of the food of lions and vultures. We shall recover our sound reason only if we shall separate ourselves from the herd—the very fact of the approbation of the multitude is a proof of the unsoundness of the opinion or practice. Let us do what is best, not what is customary. Let us love temperance—let us be just—let us refrain from bloodshed.

SENECA c. 4BC–65 AD
Roman philosopher and playwright

April 7

It is a vulgar error to regard meat in any form as necessary to life. All that is necessary to the human body can be supplied by the vegetable kingdom. It must be admitted as a fact beyond all question that some persons are sharper and more healthy who live on that (vegetarian) food. I know how much of the prevailing meat diet is not merely a wasteful extravagance but a source of serious evil to the consumer . . . I have been compelled by facts to accept the conclusion that more physical evil accrues to man from erroneous habits of diet than from any alcoholic drink.

SIR HENRY THOMPSON MD FRCS 1820–1904
English surgeon

April 8

We manage to swallow flesh only because we do not think of the cruel and sinful thing we do. There are many crimes which are the creation of man himself, the wrongfulness of which is put down to his divergence from habit, custom, or tradition. But cruelty is not of these. It is a fundamental sin, and admits of no arguments or nice distinctions. If only we do not allow our heart to grow callous it protects against cruelty, is always clearly heard; and yet we go on perpetrating cruelties easily, merrily, all of us—in fact, anyone who does not join in is dubbed a crank . . . If, after our pity is aroused, we persist in throttling our feelings simply in order to join others in preying upon life, we insult all that is good in us. I have decided to try a vegetarian diet.

RABINDRANATH TAGORE 1861–1941
Indian poet, novelist, essayist and writer of songs; winner of Nobel prize for literature in 1913

April 9

Refrain at all times from such foods as cannot be procured without violence and oppression. For know that all the inferior Creatures when hurt do cry and send forth their complaints to their Maker or grand Fountain whence they proceeded. Be not insensible that every Creature doth bear the Image of the great Creator according to the Nature of each, and that He is the Vital Part in all things. Therefore let none take pleasure to offer violence to that Life, lest he awake the fierce wrath and bring danger to his own soul.

THOMAS TRYON 1634–1703
Pythagorean, merchant, writer
Wisdom Dictates

April 10

I see shining fish struggling within tight nets, while I hear orioles sing-
ing carefree tunes. Even trivial creatures know the difference between
freedom and bondage. Sympathy and compassion should be but natural
to the human heart.

TU FU 712-770
Chinese poet
Hsin yeuh-fu shih

April 11

As I cannot kill, I cannot authorize others to kill. Do you see? If you are
buying from a butcher you are authorizing him to kill—to kill helpless,
dumb creatures which neither you nor I could kill ourselves.

PRINCE PAUL TROUBETZKOY 1866–1938
Russian sculptor
A 'Morning Leader' interview reported in *Vegetarian Messenger* 1907

April 12

Man has followed spirituality with a deadened conscience for the last 7,000 years of known history. The simple truth that no moral life demanded by spirituality is possible if he obtains food through cruelty and killing has not received general acceptance. Food is vital to life, and if it is to be acquired by destroying living beings, man cannot be consistently spiritual.

SWAMI AVYAKTANANDA 1901–1990
Spirituality
Vedanta Movement 1969

April 13

. . . death does not always result in the immediate release from the burdens of the earth life which some people imagine. Sometimes a confused, terrified or guilty mind can chain the deceased individual's spirit to earth conditions—we call this being earth-bound.

It is a state of homeless wandering of the spirit . . . Earth-bound spirits suffer great anguish . . . they flounder in a limbo of hopeless perturbation, add to the occult darkness of the world and even attach themselves to living, but unwitting, individuals.

Just as the lost discarnate forms of man pollute the milieu in which you live, so do the earth-bound psyches of murdered animals increase the secret dementia which haunts human beings without their knowing it.

God meant all creatures to die peacefully at the end of their natural lives. It is of the utmost importance that His intentions be not frust-rated—unfortunately His laws are consistently broken in the case of animals and then you wonder why it is that your lives on earth are often fraught with depressions, phobias and unhappiness in general.

It is said in the Bible that God cannot be mocked. Give much thought to this and, in doing so, realize that animals are as much part of God as you are. It is, therefore, to your advantage to treat animals humanely lest your violation of their sacred rights returns as their violation of your sacred peace.

A Pilgrimage With The Animals (Ed. by Stanley King)
From the teachings of Dr Lascelles received through his sensitive Mr C A Simpson over a period of 33 years as a healing ministry (1925–1958)
The Seekers' Trust, Kent 1982

April 14

As families throughout Britain sit down . . . to their Easter Sunday lunch, a turkey roast from Bernard Matthews will be a popular choice. The biggest turkey processor in Britain, Mr Matthews is something of a household name . . .

He had already declined to show me round either a Matthews turkey farm or production unit, on the basis that the nearest one he could show me was 40 miles away . . . (The Witchingham Factory, where, to quote one local, 'turkeys go in one side and come out the other end in many forms', is within walking distance.)

The first stumbling block was environmental impact. 'What has the environment got to do with food?' he asked. This coyness forestalled some specific questions that I wanted to put to him: the matter of the two successful prosecutions against his company in 1990 . . . (for polluting two rivers) . . .

We moved on to safer, more predictable ground. 'What has the way I rear my turkeys (I've got nothing to hide) got to do with food?' Some consumer groups are anxious about modern turkey rearing methods, I countered . . . Clearly, Mr Matthews saw welfare issues as way off limits, though in a faxed answer, he said all his staff cared about the turkeys.

The welfare groups' misgivings about the turkey industry as a whole relate to the well documented, but legal, practices such as artificial insemination of birds by methods that turn the strongest stomach, the aggressive and mutually destructive behaviour induced in these instinctively wild birds when kept in intensive conditions—which in themselves entail a seven per cent mortality rate—and slaughtering practice such as hanging heavy birds upside down for up to six minutes while awaiting death.

JOANNA BLYTHMAN 1956–
British journalist specializing in food
The Independent 30th March 1991

April 15

Farming today is pure business, the sentiment attached to it in past years no longer exists and anyone who has any knowledge of the industry will be well aware that there are many breaches of current legislation. Evidence of the new killer diseases often results in the affected cattle being passed quickly for illegal slaughter and the remains rapidly integrated into the mainstream of flesh foods.

What is the possible alternative? The luxurious gifts of the earth, with exotic herbs and spices . . . A regular intake of raw fruit and vegetables will cleanse and enrich the blood, bringing physical and mental health at all ages and freedom from the ever present worry of the killer diseases. The abundant gifts of the land invite the human race to become a compassionate and caring partner in the great work of creation, and in the present circumstances this is the only alternative.

PHILIP L PICK 1910–1992
President of the Jewish Vegetarian Society UK; editor of *Jewish Vegetarian* 1966–1992; surveyor and architect
The Jewish Vegetarian Sept 1990

∾ ∾

April 16

The greatest way to celebrate God's creation is of course through love and respect. As our sages conclude from the verse in Psalm 135: 'God is good to all and his compassion is on all his creatures', that we must emulate his ways.

In truth, Judaism is both Particular and Universal . . . Accordingly, the very concept of Jewish vegetarianism expresses this authentic combination within Judaism, in which commitment to the Jewish people is not at the expense of universal commitment but, on the contrary, should serve as a stimulus and catalyst for such.

RABBI DAVID ROSEN
President of J V S, Israel
The Jewish Vegetarian September 1990

April 17

Secrecy serves to conceal the details of the horror from all but those who must participate in it to keep the cogs of the machinery running smoothly . . . the public is not generally admitted to the window-less 'factory farm' buildings, . . . which are scattered in out-of-the-way locations . . . slaughterhouses, located off the beaten track, are also closed to public scrutiny . . .

All of this secrecy is necessary to keep the system intact. In the case of animal slavery, the outsiders are not mere spectators, as mentioned by Hallie (talking about human slavery), but are complicit in the system. Nearly everyone feeds quite literally upon the fruits of this cruelty. In order to go on doing so, we must be able to disassociate the actual producers—the animals themselves—from their 'products': meat, milk, eggs, leather, fur etc. In order to go on with 'business as usual' and not disrupt their life in any 'major' way, it is necessary for the average person to be able to smilingly purchase that carton of milk and picture a happy cow frolicking with her calf in a field. When buying what is euphemistically termed 'beef', this person must picture, if *anything*, a large beefy brainless sort of creature who doesn't even have the sense to notice he's alive.

MARJORIE SPIEGEL
The Dreaded Comparison—Human and Animal Slavery
Heretic Books 1988

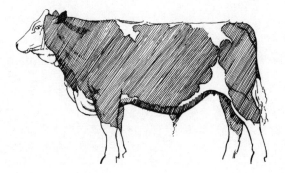

April 18

I know what the caged bird feels, alas!
When the sun is bright on the upland slopes;
When the wind stirs soft through springing grass,
And the river flows like a stream of glass;
When the first bird sings and the first bud opes,
And the faint perfume from its chalice steals—
I know what the caged bird feels!

I know why the caged bird beats his wing
Till its blood is red on the cruel bars;
For he must fly back to his perch and cling
When he fain would be on the bough a-swing;
And a pain still throbs in the old, old scars
And they pulse again with a keener sting—
I know why he beats his wing!

I know why the caged bird sings, alone,
When his wing is bruised and his bosom sore—
When he beats his bars and he would be free;
It is not a carol of joy or glee,
But a prayer that he sends from his heart's deep core,
But a plea, that upward to heaven he flings—
I know why the caged bird sings!

PAUL LAWRENCE DUNBAR 1872–1906
American poet and writer, son of two runaway slaves
Sympathy

April 19

Again we have been distressed by the wholesale barbarity of tourists who seem to make Florida animals mere marks for unskilled hunters to practice upon, and who go everywhere maiming, wounding and killing poor birds and beasts that they do not even stop to pick up, and shoot in mere wantonness. Last year we exerted ourselves to get a law passed protecting the birds of Florida which were being trapped and carried off by thousands to die in miserable little cages—veritable slave ships—I for my part am ready to do anything that can benefit the cause.

HARRIET BEECHER STOWE 1811–1896
American writer, author of *Uncle Tom's Cabin*
From a letter 6 November 1877 to Henry Bergh, Founder of the first US Humane Society

April 20

. . . Today's chicken farms are not really 'farms' anymore, but should accurately be called 'chicken factories'. Factories, because the chickens live their whole lives inside buildings entirely devoid of natural light. The day of the barnyard is long gone. There are no barns and no yards in today's mechanized world of poultry production, only assembly lines, conveyor belts, and fluorescent lights. Factories, because these proud and sensitive creatures are treated strictly as merchandise, with utter contempt for their spirits, with not a trace of feeling or compassion for the fact that they are living, breathing animals. Factories, because the chickens are systematically deprived of every conceivable expression of their natural urges.

JOHN ROBBINS
Diet For A New America
Stillpoint USA 1987

April 21

The writer knows of a hen which is six years old now. A farmer friend
of his brought it with a dozen of her sisters from a battery farm some
years ago—poor, featherless, demented things. They then were unable
to perch, and stared vacantly at the new experience called 'grass'. It was
something out of this world for her, until taught by other freer cousins
the joys of free-range. This hen, called 'One-tail', because she only ever
did grow one feather in her tail, now enters the house through the
cat-flap and challenges the cat to its dinner.

The emotions of the animals and of human beings are, no doubt, the
same, even though we may differ in our respective necessities and in
degree. They feel pain and joy, they fear and feel relief, they experience
an advanced sense of fun—all just as we do.

AL-HAFIZ BA Masri   1914–1992
Former Imam of Woking Mosque, England; campaigner for the respect and
welfare of animals
Islamic Concern For Animals
Athene Trust 1987

ᜑ ᜒ

April 22

The battery chickens I have observed seem to lose their minds about
the time they would normally be weaned by their mothers and off in
the woods chasing grasshoppers of their own account. Yes, literally, the
battery becomes a gallinaceous madhouse.

R BEDICHECK
Adventures with a Texas Naturalist
University of Texas Press 1961

April 23

Vedantic Ethics based on the Unity of Life and the feeling of the self in all and all in the self is an extended Ethics covering all living beings. Every living being has the same love of life and the right to exist without molestation. The human race has been a race of demons in its behaviour towards sub-human creatures . . . Vedanta teaches us not to molest them for food, dress, fashion, sport and research. It is a great experience to feel deeply the Oneness of Life.

SWAMI AVYAKTANANDA 1901–1990
The Vedantic Manifesto For India

April 24

Permission to kill and eat animals was only granted as a result of man's evil and was accompanied with a curse.

(Genesis 9:5)

Flesh foods are now the product of obscene cruelty, and contravene Tzaar baal chaim. 98% of all meat and poultry, kosher and non-kosher, comes from factory farms, contrary to many provisions of the Torah.

Nowhere in the Tenach is there a promise of flesh foods of any kind as a reward for keeping the commandments. The promise is always the gift of produce of the vines, the gardens and the fields.

From: *Why a Jewish Vegetarian Society?*

April 25

I don't know what shall be the destinies of those responsible for the animal factories of today. But regardless of the future, it is already sadly true that they live in a heartless world. Treating animals like machines, they are profoundly separated from nature, deeply alienated from kinship with life. They are already in a kind of hell.

If we buy and eat the products of this system of food production, are we not colluding with them in creating this hell?

Is that how we want to vote with our lives?

JOHN ROBBINS
Diet For A New America
Stillpoint USA 1987

≈ ≈

April 26

There is a destiny that makes us brothers,
None goes his way alone—
All that we send into the lives of others
Comes back into our own.

AUTHOR UNKNOWN

April 27

If animals are to redress the harm done to them by adverse influence, then time and patience are necessary, but many people have shown just how successful individual attempts may be. Lady Dowding managed to train one of her cats not to kill. Robertson was a marmalade tom . . . But Robertson was a bird hunter. Muriel and Hugh Dowding decided to send him to Coventry every time he caught one. He was very upset at being ignored—though his food would still be put down for him—and would do anything to attract their attention. In fact, his antics would send them off into another room to hide their laughter. But Robertson did learn that he was doing wrong. Eventually they watched him lying beside the bird bath, birds bathing happily alongside him.

REBECCA HALL
Animals Are Equal
Wildwood House 1980; Rider 1988; PKP 1993

April 28

In the earliest years of life, and at a time when the mind receives its most indelible impressions, we find that the child is taught both by precept and observation that the *natural* destiny of most of the creatures it sees around it, many of them perhaps, such as birds, rabbits or lambs, its loved playmates and companions, is to be killed and eaten by himself and his fellows. The child is taught that man's superior powers confer on him the right to utilize them as he will and if the child is horrified and repelled by the sight or smell of their flesh, or at the idea of thus feasting on the bodies of his friends, compliance with custom is insisted on under the plea that such food is 'necessary' to him for the maintenance of health and strength. And in our Western Christian countries he would be assured that God had sent them for this express purpose; nay, that He had definitely commanded such use of them, and the child's contumacy in thus refusing the 'good gifts of the Creator' would be surely rebuked. This is an assertion which in effect has doubtless been often made with equal truth and logic by the South Sea Cannibal anent the missionaries newly landed on his shores . . . What course of training the plastic and developing mind and moral nature (enforced as it is by ever present practical object lessons, and appealing as it does so subtly to his pride of position as 'lord of creation') could be more insidious and at the same time more effectual . . . For destroying the ideas of the sacredness of life and reverence for its giver, for blunting finer moral feelings, for fostering and confirming an egotism, careless of the lives and sufferings of others so long as self is ministered to, for inculcating the unholy lesson that might constitutes 'right' and for preparing its subject for an extended application of this principle against his sub-human fellows for purposes of amusement, spoilation, or scientific research, or against his fellow men in depression, violence and war.

Robert H Perks md frcs
English surgeon and first Honorary Secretary of the Order of the Cross
The Moral Responsibility of Flesh Eaters
Herald of The Cross Vol I 1905

April 29

Raising a child on a healthy vegetarian diet is one of the most concrete actions of love a parent can make. On a physical level, exposure to healthy foods allows optimal growth and helps prevent disease. On a social level, following a healthy vegetarian diet is a basic step toward increasing the chance that our planet will survive and flourish.

Vegetarianism is, for me, the ideal parenting medium. It allows me to nurture a healthy child and instil him with important social values. The concept of connection between all living things is essential to vegetarianism. It leads me to a continuing interaction with others, widening my own knowledge of the world which I then share with my son . . . As my understanding of vegetarianism deepens, my ability to relate in a healthy way to my family, and to the world at large, also grows.

SHARON YNTENA 1951–
American vegetarian farmer, child development specialist, technical writer and author
Vegetarian Children
Thorsons 1989

∾ ∾

April 30

Marine Captain Alan Jones of Quantico, Virginia, is a vegetarian: Although crippled by polio when he was five years old, Jones is another candidate for the world's fittest man and has amassed a record of physical accomplishments unmatched by any human being that ever lived. Not only does he hold the world record for continuous situps (17,003), but in one particular fifteen month period he accomplished possibly the most remarkable array of physical achievements ever attained by a human being.

JOHN ROBBINS
Diet For A New America
Stillpoint USA 1987

May 1

For the sake of some little mouthful of flesh, we deprive a soul of the sun and light and of that proportion of life and time it had been born into the world to enjoy.

PLUTARCH c. 46–120 AD
A Greek biographer and priest of the Delphic Apollo; one of the most erudite men of his age—as judged by his writings

May 2

You who are innocent, what have you done worthy of death?

RICHARD OF WYCHE 1197–1253
Bishop of Chichester on observing animals being killed for food

May 3

The tender hearted Hindoo would turn from our tables with abhorrence. To him our feasts are the nefarious repasts of Polyphonus; while we contemplate with surprise his absurd clemency, and regard his superstitious mercy as an object of merriment and contempt.

JOHN OSWALD d. 1793
Scottish soldier-poet
The Cry of Nature or An appeal to Mercy and Justice on Behalf of The Persecuted Animals
London 1791

May 4

Do not degrade and beastatize your body by making it a burial place for the carcasses of innocent brute animals, some healthy, some diseased and all violently murdered. It is impossible for us to take into our stomachs putrefying, corrupting, and diseased animal substances, without becoming obnoxious to horrors, dejections, remorse, and inquietudes of mind, and to foul bodily diseases, swellings, pains, weaknesses, sores, corruptions, and premature death.

DR GRAHAM
From *On the Conduct of Man to the Inferior Animals*
An anthology made by George Nicholson, Yorkshire printer and vegetarian
Manchester 1797

May 5

I will not kill nor hurt any living creature needlessly, nor destroy any beautiful thing; but will strive to save and comfort all gentle life, and perfect all natural beauty upon the earth.

JOHN RUSKIN 1819–1900
English writer and critic and scholar of varied interests, who espoused the cause of social and economic reform
Fifth Rule for the Society of St George

May 6

The unnatural eating of flesh-meats is as polluting as the heathen worship of devils, with its sacrifices and its unpure feasts, through participation in which a man becomes a fellow-eater with devils.

CLEMENS ALEXANDRINUS second century AD
Promoted Christianity
Clementine Homilies

⊲ ⊳

May 7

The church so hated these good people (the Albigenses—an 'heretical' Christian sect of 13th Century France) whose Christ-like compassion was such a judgement on its own pagan and anti-Christian violence, that their vegetarian habits were not only represented as signs of a diabolical heresy, but were also used as a means to detect and convict them. For when prisoners were taken, sheep were led to them and knives provided for their butchery. Those who refused to kill the animals were burnt at the stake, and the majority did refuse since to take sentient life violated the very basis of their faith.

ESMÉ WYNNE-TYSON 1898–1972
English writer
The Philosophy of Compassion
Centaur Press 1962

May 8

It is evident that those who are necessitated by their profession to trifle with the sacredness of life, and think lightly of the agonies of living beings, are unfit for the benevolence and justice which is required for the performance of the offices of civilized society. They are by necessity brutal, coarse, turbulent and sanguinary. Their habits form an admirable apprenticeship to the more wasting wickedness of war, in which men are lured to mangle and munch their fellow beings by thousands, that tyrants and countries may profit. How can he be expected to preserve a vivid sensibility to the benevolent sympathies of a nature who is familiar with carnage, agony and groans? The very sight of animals in the fields who are destined to the axe must encourage obduracy if it fails to awaken compassion. The butchering of harmless animals cannot fail to produce much of that spirit of unique and hideous exultation in which news of a victory is related although punctured by the massacre of a hundred thousand men. If the use of animal food be in consequence, subversive to the peace of human society, how unwarrantable is the injustice and barbarity which is exercised towards these miserable victims.

PERCY BYSSHE SHELLEY 1792–1822
English poet and radical thinker
On Vegetable System of Diet

◈ ◈

May 9

Vegetarianism is my religion. I became a consistent vegetarian some twenty years ago . . . When a human kills an animal for food, he is neglecting his own hunger for justice. Man prays for mercy, but is unwilling to extend it to others. Why should man then expect mercy from God? It's unfair to expect something that you are not willing to give. It is inconsistent . . .

To be a vegetarian is to disagree—to disagree with the course of things today. Nuclear power, starvation, cruelty—we must make a statement against these things. Vegetarianism is my statement. And I think it's a strong one.

ISAAC BASHEVIS SINGER 1904–1992
American writer, winner of Nobel Prize for Literature 1978
In Preface to *Food For the Spirit* (Steven Rosen)
Bala Books USA 1987

May 10

Vegetarianism is a way of life that we should all move toward for economic survival, physical well-being and spiritual integrity.

FATHER THOMAS BARRY
Catholic priest, founder of Riverdale Centre of Religious Research; former Director, History of Religion Program, Fordham University, New York

∽. ∾

May 11

For that which befalleth the sons of men, befalleth beasts, even one thing befalleth them: As one dieth, so dieth the other. Yes, they have all one breath. So that a man hath no pre-eminence above a beast—for all is vanity.

Ecclesiastes 3:19
A book of the Old Testament. c. 3rd Century BC

∽. ∾

May 12

Forbear, O Mortals, to taint your bodies with forbidden food;
Corn have we; the boughs bend under a load of fruit;
Our vines abound in swelling grapes; our fields with wholesome
        herbs,
Whereof those of a cruder kind may be softened and mellowed by fire.
Nor is milk denied us, nor honey smelling of the fragrant thyme;
Earth is lavish of her riches, and teems with kindly stores
Providing without slaughter or bloodshed, for all manner of delights.

PYTHAGORAS 540-510 BC
From *Metamorphosis* by Ovid

May 13

It is my view that the vegetarian manner of living, by its purely physical effect on the human temperament, would most beneficially influence the lot of mankind.

ALBERT EINSTEIN 1879–1955
German-Swiss American physicist. Winner of Nobel Prize 1921

May 14

Everything is related. Whatever happens now to animals will eventually happen to man.

INDIRA GANDHI 1917–1985
Daughter of Jawaharlal Nehru, Indian statesman. Former prime minister of India

May 15

Flesh foods are not the best nourishment for human beings and were not the food of our primitive ancestors. They are secondary or secondhand products, since all food comes originally from the vegetable kingdom. There is nothing necessary or desirable for human nutrition to be found in meats or flesh foods which is not found in and derived from vegetable products.

A dead cow or sheep lying in a pasture is recognized as carrion. The same sort of carcass dressed and hung up in a butcher's stall passes as food. Careful microscopic examination may show little or no difference between the fence corner carcass and the butcher's shop carcass. Both are swarming with colon germs and redolent with putrefaction.

JOHN HARVEY KELLOGG 1852–1943
American surgeon, founder of Battle Creek Sanitorium; Seventh Day Adventist (By 1906 there were 7,000 patients being cared for at Battle Creek where fresh fruits and vegetables were the important foods)

May 16

THE COWS ARE GONE

It is called 'the fattening field' and the cattle fenced and friendly look
up to the lane at people walking by.
Christmas is gone and the fattening field is silent now.
Not a single cow; but a prattle of fat people in the town.
And there's no Happy New Year for the cattle.
An empty twilit field stands still,
And the twilight zone of the pub is full—to bursting
with red-faces standing at the bar.
It's a good night out with laughter.
Addled and fuddled they'll muddle home after
they've slaughtered nine pints and a rump.

I watched them play when they lived,
munching away at the grass.
But they too were green and hadn't seen the lie in the farmer's eye.
They stood at the hedge at the field's edge,
and I touched their noses through the branches to feel their sedate
    dignity.
To open a gate to some new Elysian field.

We live at death's edge,
And imagine we defy it—blind to the lie,
and the least little hatred which sharp as a knife
would cut us too out of this green paradise.

REBECCA HALL
1991

◈ ◈

May 17

As long as human society continues to allow cows to be regularly
killed in slaughterhouses, there cannot be any question of peace and
prosperity.

A C BHAKTIVEDANTA SWAMI PRABHUPADA
Hindu religion. Founder-Acharya of the International Society for Krishna
consciousness

May 18

Thanks be to God: since I gave up flesh and wine, I have been delivered from all physical ills.

JOHN WESLEY 1703–1791
English evangelist and theologian, founder of Methodism

~ ~

May 19

When an animal is slaughtered, the waste products normally taken away by the animal's bloodstream are retained in the decaying flesh. Meat-eaters absorb into their own bodies the toxic wastes that would otherwise have been expelled from the animal's body as urine. Dr Owen S Parrett, in his paper, 'Why I Don't Eat Meat', notes that when steak is boiled waste appears as a soluble extract in the form of beef tea—which closely resembles urine when chemically analyzed.

STEVEN ROSEN 1955–
Food For The Spirit
Bala Books 1987

~ ~

May 20

All the bloodshed caused by the warlike disposition of Napoleon is as nothing compared to the myriads of persons who have sunk into their graves through a misplaced confidence in the value of beef tea.

DR MILNER FOTHERGILL 1841–1888
Medical writer

May 21

The change to a vegan-type diet may offer important advantages to health. Vegans seem to be less prone to coronary heart disease, cancer of the large bowel, diverticular disease and obesity. A vegan diet is also a cheap one. The high price of meat and fish may well encourage many to adopt this type of diet. Such a change, besides saving money, might also have the far more significant effect of saving life.

T A B SANDERS BSC PHD
Vegan Nutrition
Department of Nutritional Food Science. Queen Elizabeth College, University of London

∾ ∽

May 22

One thousand acres of soyabeans yield 1,124 pounds of usable protein. One thousand acres of rice yield 938 pounds of usable protein. One thousand acres of corn yield 1,009 pounds of usable protein. One thousand acres of wheat yield 1,043 pounds of usable protein.

. . . One thousand acres of soyabeans, corn, rice or wheat, *when fed to a steer*, will yield only about 125 pounds of usable protein.

PHILIP HANDLER
Science, Food and Man's Future
Borden Review of Nutrition Research Vol 31 No 1 Jan-Mar 1971

May 23

Never forget that what you *eat* and what you *think* is what you *are*. The food taken into your body is what gradually . . . slowly but surely . . . forms your thought patterns. And your thoughts, both conscious and sub-conscious, are in absolute control of your body's health or lack of it.

LINDA GOODMAN
American astrologer and writer
Linda Goodman's Star Signs
Pan Books 1987

๛ ๛

May 24

Any integrated view of life as a whole will reveal to us the connection between the individual's food and his behaviour towards others, and through a process of ratiocination which is not fantastic, we cannot but arrive at the conclusion that the only means of escaping the hydrogen bomb is to escape the (type of) mentality which has produced it, and the only way to escape that mentality is to cultivate respect for all life, life in all forms, under all conditions. It is only another name for vegetarianism.

DR RAJENDRA PRASAD   1884–1963
First President of the Republic of India
Searchlight

May 25

But Daniel purposed in his heart that he would not defile himself with the portion of the king's meat, nor with the wine which he drank: therefore he requested of the prince of the Eunuchs that he might not defile himself.

Now God had brought Daniel into favour and tender love with the prince of the Eunuchs.

And the prince of the Eunuchs said unto Daniel, I fear my lord the king, who hath appointed your meat and your drink: for why should he see your faces worse liking than the children which *are* of your sort? Then shall ye make *me* endanger my head to the king.

Then said Daniel to Mel'zar whom the prince of the Eunuchs had set after Daniel, Hananiah, Mishael and Azariah.

Prove thy servants, I beseech thee, ten days: and let them give us pulse to eat, and water to drink.

Then let our countenances be looked upon before thee, and the countenance of the children that eat of the portions of the king's meat: and as thou seest, deal with thy servants.

So he consented to them in this matter, and proved them ten days.

And at the end of ten days their countenances appeared fairer and fatter in flesh than all the children which did eat the portion of the king's meat.

Thus Mel'zar took away the portion of their meat and the wine that they should drink: and gave them pulse.

As for these four children, God gave them knowledge and skill in all learning and wisdom: and Daniel had understanding in all visions and dreams.

The Book of Daniel, Chapter 1:8–17 (The Old Testament)

May 26

Daniel 'purposed' in his heart not to defile his body with the king's unwholesome foods. This discipline preceeded what was granted in those higher powers by which he penetrated a dimension not accessible unless the vehicles of physical being and of mind be freed of dross from self-indulgences . . .

Cells that are purified by living foods of earth attract the radiance which they can bear. When the body can support Everlasting Light, the Light will fall upon the waiting ones.

MARY C FULLERSON
The Form of the Fourth
Stuart & Watkins London 1971

May 27

Wild animals become tame and are said to lick the hand of the Yogi secure in Ahimsa (non-violence). Patanjali says: 'Near him in whom non-violence has fully taken root, all beings renounce enmity.'

JAMES HEWITT
The Five Abstinences: Yoga
Patanjali: 900-800 BC (or possibly much earlier)
Indian sage who compiled the Yoga Sutras

May 28

The ideal is not to eat flesh, not to injure any living creature, for all animals are my brothers. If you can think of them as your brothers you have made a little headway towards the brotherhood of all souls, not to speak of the brotherhood of man.

SWAMI VIVEKANANDA 1862–1902
Indian spiritual teacher

May 29

Sri Ramakrishna says that the spiritual seekers should not take fish and meat . . . Sri Ramakrishna liked plain rice and vegetables to be eaten by those who were eager for spirituality. According to him, complicated cooking with vegetables, fish, meat and rich things was not good in spiritual life. Once he said that his ideal was to be like a Brahmin widow who would live in a cottage with a little plot of land for growing vegetables.

SWAMI AVYAKTANANDA 1901–1990
Sri Ramakrishna For All—As I Understand Him Now (1988)
19th Century Indian teacher

May 30

It was not necessary that the animal which of all others is most akin to wisdom, namely man, should . . . change his nature into something resembling the ferocity of wild beasts; on which account . . . those who have any regard for temperance entirely abstain from such things, eating only vegetables and herbs, and the fruits of trees, as the most delicious and wholesome food.

PHILO JUDEUS first century AD
Alexandrian philosopher
Fragments of the Lost Works

May 31

Taking away the lives of animals, in order to convert them into food does great violence to the principles of benevolence and compassion. This appears from the frequent hard-heartedness and cruelty found amongst those persons whose occupations engaged them in destroying animal life, as well as from the uneasiness which others feel in beholding the butchery of animals.

DAVID HARTLEY 1705–1757
Philosopher
Observations of Man (1748)

June 1

A wealthy English landowner went each day to feed his doves near a barn. One day, he saw a large rat fill its mouth with grain and scamper off to a neighbouring coach house. It repeated this performance several times and so he decided to follow it. There he found a lame dove eating the corn brought to it by the rat. The rat, never staying, would run away as soon as its task was completed.

From *The Animals Magazine*
Journal of the PDSA (Peoples' Dispensary For Sick Animals UK)

June 2

Roy Plomley: 'Could you catch your own food—would you be able to fish?'
Tom Keating (painter): 'No, I wouldn't do that. I don't like killing.'

TOM KEATING
Famous copyist of the Masters
Desert Island Discs
BBC Radio 4 1983

☙ ☙

June 3

Babs Williams's cats Jon Jon, Jasper and Josh never caught birds. She hated the idea of them hunting and managed to bring out the opposite urge in them . . . These three never had to be taught gentleness . . . Jasper, Jon Jon and Josh would walk among the birds when she threw out food for them in winter with no fuss or ruffled feathers.

Nor has her present cat, Blossom, ever caught a bird. When a young thrush flew through the window into her room one day, Blossom watched it and when Babs came in, mewed at her as if asking what could be done about this frightened little creature.

REBECCA HALL
Animals are Equal
Wildwood House 1980; Rider 1988; PKP 1993

June 4

It is from [the] vegan ideal that the healing of the world can come . . .
My medical practice is based upon pure vegetarian nutrition. Daily, I
see the health-enhancing powers of a diet free from the flesh and milk
of animals . . . The vegan ideal lives in our hearts and within our vision
of a kinder, gentler world . . . we each can take responsibility for our
corner and make that part as peaceful as can be. A safer, greener, saner
world is ours for the growing. May the vegan spirit . . . kindle the flame
of love and understanding in hearts around the globe. If we all love
enough, we will see a brighter day.

MICHAEL KLAPER MD
American doctor, nutritionist and educator
A lecture to the Seventh International Vegan Festival, Spain 1993

June 5

I have been inside abattoirs; and I can assure you it is terrible to witness
the sufferings of the creatures before they are killed, and to witness the
process by which they are killed, and the effect of such upon those who
kill them. If only men and women could recognize that the creatures are
also little Spiritual children of the FATHER-MOTHER.

Many of them are not little in their fury, but they are little in their
estate . . .

The spirit of war that obtains throughout the world is generated and
nurtured, and in a sense it is almost inspired by the conflict of men with
the creatures. The slaying of the creatures is the carrying out of the spirit
of war . . . If everyone loved truly, there would be no more slaying of the
creatures.

REV JOHN TODD FERRIER 1855–1943
Herald of the Cross Vol XII 1938
An open letter to the children
Order of the Cross

June 6

UN Day is perhaps an occasion when we should stop and give thanks for our freedom from war. A time to consider those people who know nothing of lasting peace, who starve, who are oppressed and are exploited. The International Meat Trade is a wasteful trade; where people need grain for their own consumption, instead this is fed to animals, which in turn satisfy the craving of meat-eating man in the affluent areas of the world. By adopting a meat-free diet, we boycott the international meat trade, and help ease social injustice throughout the world.

Declaration for 24th October: UN *Day*
The Vegetarian Society of the UK

June 7

The doctrine which is that of the modern school of abstainers from flesh, was that of the Magi who initiated Daniel; of the Therapeuts, who drew their origin and their knowledge from Egyptian adepts; of the Buddhists; of the Nazarites, who counted Jesus among their number; of the Essenes, who produced his friend and companion, John the Baptist; of the Ebionites and Recluses; of the Exponents of the Christian 'Gnosis', who kept alive and bequeathed to us through the Neo Platonists that spirit of understanding, that 'seeing eye' and 'hearing ear' possible only in their completeness to men of pure heart and life.

In extolling this pure heart, in advocating this clean and blameless life, in indicating this perfect way, we imitate the illuminati of all ages.

ANNA KINGSFORD MD 1846–1888
The Perfect Way in Diet
Kegan Paul 1906

June 8

But they of ancient times, justly called the Age of Gold,
Content with the fruit of their trees and the herbs of earth, stained not
their lips with blood;
Then might the birds in safety traverse the airy expanse and the hare
rove fearless over field and moor,
Nor were even the credulous fish beguiled by the deceitful hook;
Snares and treachery were unknown, no dread of fraud disturbed
the mind,
all things were full of peace.

PYTHAGORAS 6th century BC (fl. 540-510)
The Samian sage, ascribed by Ovid

June 9

The moral considerations press on us two sides with irresistible force.
The aggregate of animal suffering in the cause of the table is simply
appalling, and there is nothing for it but to shut our eyes and ears.
The life of an ox from the pasture to the butcher's shop will not bear
telling. One night on a cattle steamer would be enough for most of us.
The table . . . brutalizes and degrades a multitude of men whom society
employs and shuns . . . And so all our ideas of life and its dignity and
significance suffer.

A 'PARISH PARSON'
From a letter in a serial publication for February 1881

June 10

The first lessons a butcher's apprentice generally receives from the journeyman is how to torture the animals which are to be slaughtered; and they are frequently allowed to use the axe before they are well able to lift it, to the indescribable agony of the poor beast. Again, when a slaughterman is in a hurry to get away he is not particular about skinning the animal before it is dead. This I have seen occur daily, where there has been a large amount of work to be done.

From a letter of a journeyman butcher
Staffordshire Daily Sentinel June 17 1879

June 11

Habit blunts the sensibilities of men who are not naturally cruel; and besides, there are many people who never realize the fact that 'brute beasts' can be made to suffer at all. People who would look with horror at the torture of a man, complacently behold the suffering of his poor relations. We are afraid that the pleasure of the table would be greatly impaired if the guests knew the whole history of the manner in which the steaming joint or the daintily-served chicken even had been prepared for their use. 'Tis enough to make vegetarians of us all even to think of it.'

EDITOR'S COMMENT
Staffordshire Daily Sentinel June 1879

June 12

I would call attention to the description given of the animals in the Golden Age, spoken of in the prophetic visions—an age when all things shall be restored—in which they are depicted as living in a state of innocence and harmlessness. The obvious inference from these descriptions being that man and the lower animals are so far essentially one in their physical and mental natures that their response to psychic and spiritual influence only differs in degree, and this is also in harmony with our noblest thoughts concerning the Divine Compassion flowing out to and embracing all creatures.

ROBERT H PERKS MD
Herald of the Cross. Vol I 1905
The Order of the Cross

June 13

MEAT
(On seeing some sheep driven into this town—Dorking—one summer day)

Coming down the busy street
On little tired, stumbling feet,
Here, O Christians, comes your meat.

Dusty, dirty—one is lame.
He is driven just the same,
Driven to his Gethsemane,
That you may have lamb chops for tea.

Mouths are open, panting wide;
You may see the tongues inside
Tongues you shall tomorrow eat
Rejoice, O Christians, here is meat!

ELSBETH DOUGLAS REID
Crimes Against Creation (edited by Marie Dreyfus)

June 14

One night . . . I found myself leaving the physical body but instead of the soaring upward motion, I had a heavy weighted feeling, as if I were freed to travel in a horizontal position, and suddenly found myself in a narrow, dark street . . . the ground was covered with mud and slime. Gloomy buildings like stables, huddled against each other . . . here and there I saw a wider opening . . . I looked in and saw that the yard was crowded with animals—bullocks, pigs and sheep—dead, and yet alive. I *knew* they were dead, but I could see that they were alive too. They moved very slightly, many lay on the ground. I understood at once . . . that they had just been slaughtered.

I pulled myself together with tremendous effort . . . The place and everything in it was so horrible . . . I noticed that there was a great difference in the *substance* of this plane, compared with that of the planes where I had seen ordinary discarnate human life . . . it was indeed most dreadful and repulsive . . .

Its misery was due to the tremendous slaughtering of animals for food that takes place daily . . . In the very air . . . was a most definite feeling of terrible fear, suffering, and blind resentment . . . it had affected the spiritual and mental atmosphere of the earth, and had a bad effect on human life and progress.

GLADYS OSBORNE LEONARD 1882–1968
English spiritualist and medium
My Life in Two Worlds
Cassell & Co Ltd 1931

June 15

With regard to flesh-eating . . . many serious diseases come from this loathsome habit of devouring dead bodies; man is not naturally inclined to be carnivorous and therefore this abominable food is not suited to him; men are stronger and better on a vegetable diet; the eating of dead bodies leads to indulgence in drink and increases animal passions in man . . . men who eat flesh are responsible for the sins and degradation caused in the slaughterhouse; carnivorous diet is fatal to real development; and produces the most undesirable results on both astral and mental bodies; man's duty towards the animal kingdom is not to slaughter it recklessly, but to assist in its evolution . . .

No man needs these things, and to take them is just a matter of selfish indulgence. Most men commit this act in ignorance of the harm that it is doing; but remember, to continue to commit it when the truth is known is a crime.

C W LEADBEATER 1847–1934
One of the founders of the Theosophical Movement in India and Britain
The Hidden Side of Things
Theosophical Publishing House 1919

June 16

But the spiritual Empire of Pity cannot be limited to the region of man alone; it must extend wherever suffering is; it must embrace all living things . . . now in this new age, its borders are being enlarged. Pity is whispering into the hearts of men a new story of her beautiful kindness; of her tender ministry of peace . . . and man, in his most divine moments when the clamours of lust and appetite are stilled, must perforce listen; and though today his ears be dull and his understanding closed, after many days and many sorrows he will hear and understand.

Man still inflicts perpetual suffering on those weaker creatures . . . he breeds and slaughters large numbers of them that he may be gratified with the smell and taste of their roasted flesh. He thinks his God has created them for his special pleasure and to serve him as food, and that he is therefore performing the will of his God in doing them violence . . . and Pity waits and watches.

And now . . . man is groping . . . for a fuller understanding and expression of that Perfect love which he has always worshipped but not comprehended . . . kill not, neither do thou eat the fruit of violence, but protect all creatures with kindness . . .

Blessed is he who stills the brutish voice of desire within him, and follows the gentle pleading of Pity, knowing that desire is selfish, and that Pity is divine.

JAMES ALLEN
The Bryngoleu Cookery Book 1906

June 17

. . . During the Unfallen days . . . the Creatures . . . were not driven over by the cruelty of man. Just as there were no Carnivores in the world at that time, so there were no cruel men and women who loved to sport with the lives of the Creatures and have joy in taking the gift of life from them in sport, or in slaying them for food. There was no such thing on the Planet, and it was quite foreign to the Planetary manifestation. You could not imagine such a state of things existing in relation to the Divine Love and Wisdom . . .

The Creatures were happy. Why should not the Creatures be happy? Why should they fear man? Why should they run away from man instead of coming to him as to one who is their king and friend? A true king is lovely to his subjects. He is not a dominating mind, but a great regal heart. So should men have been to the Creatures.

REV JOHN TODD FERRIER 1855–1943
Herald of the Cross Vol XII 1938
The Order of the Cross

June 18

Animals are accorded no enforceable rights under English law: they are permitted no advocate, no tribunal will entertain a plea on their behalf; and no injunction may be sought to prevent their suffering.

But no earthly law will stop their voiceless processional to the slaughterhouses; only voluntary obedience by every man and woman to the one true Universal Law that proclaims all life as equal, sacred and inviolable.

MATTHEW HALL 1967–
Barrister-at-Law
A statement written for this book

June 19

That mankind in the present stage of *polished* life acts in direct violation of the principles of justice, mercy, tenderness, sympathy and humanity, in the practice of eating flesh is obvious. To take away the life of any happy being, to commit acts of depredation and outrage, and to abandon every refined feeling and sensibility, is to degrade the human kind beneath its professed dignity of character; but to *devour* or eat any animal is an additional violation of these principles, because it is the *extreme* of brutal ferocity. Such is the conduct of the most savage of wild beasts, and of the most uncultivated and barbarous of our own species. Where is the person who with calmness, can bear himself compared in disposition to a lion, a hyena, a tiger, or a wolf? And yet he is exactly similar in his disposition.

GEORGE NICHOLSON 1760–1825
Yorkshire printer and vegetarian

June 20

It is not, however, because animals have souls and continue after death that we are bound to be just and merciful to them, but because we ourselves have souls of which the principles of justice and mercy are the very life-blood, and which we degrade and destroy by being unjust and unmerciful. Suffer as the animals may through our ill-treatment of them, we ourselves suffer yet more thereby. So that the notion, so prevalent, that humanity—meaning men and women—can be benefited by methods involving the ill-treatment of animals is utterly absurd and false. Humanity cannot be benefited by aught that is, by its very nature, subversive of humanity.

ANNA KINGSFORD MD 1846–1888
The Credo of Christendom
Watkins 1916

June 21

It is significant of the latent and secret consciousness of the *unspiritual* nature of the products of the slaughterhouse even in the Western World, that in the 'liturgies' of 'sources' of the Christian Churches, wherever food is prayed for or whenever thanks is returned for it, there is (as it seems), a natural shrinking from mention of that which is obtained only by cruelty and bloodshed: and it is the 'kindly fruits of the earth' which represent the legitimate dietary wants of the petitioners.

HAROLD WILLIAMSON MA
Herald of the Cross Vol II 1906
The Order of The Cross

June 22

When I informed my friends that I was going on a tour of India, Pakistan and Bangladesh, I was told by almost all of them that I was betaking myself to a mission impossible . . . that people in the East would not be interested in the animal or environmental problems . . .

However, the subsequent 109 days allayed my qualms, as I trekked through more than twenty cities of the subcontinent . . . some of the public meetings had audiences of more than 500 . . .

(These) people . . . are currently under attack by the consumer orientated economics of the so-called developed countries . . . and are being encouraged to throw centuries-old moral values overboard in the name of progress and civilization. During my childhood . . . some 75 years ago, a meat-eating Hindu used to be considered a miscreant. Today, by and large, eating meat is fast becoming a status symbol of civility and vigour. Paradoxically . . . I came across quite a few Muslims who had become vegetarian . . . they now get a chance to see, right under their noses, the inhumane conditions in their abattoirs. The whole chain of the meat trade, starting from the farm, passing through the various channels of transport and auction etc, and ending up in the slaughter houses is a stigma on the face of human civilization.

. . . While I saw all this and much more with dismay, I was at the same time heartened to see a wave of protest, especially among the younger generation, against this kind of dehumanization of our society.

AL HAFIZ MASRI
Agscene No 99 May/June 1990

June 23

It takes a certain skill to be a slaughterman and the approach is not so much technical as philosophical. It's an amoral process that needs detachment to run parallel with responsibility in the execution of one's duties. You'll also get to learn to live with that smell . . . a smell which seems to permeate your clothes, even your family will get to know and have to get used to living with it. It taints your senses.

Halal and Kosher butchers hire the abattoir on Saturdays to ritually sacrifice their food with the aid of a quick prayer and a blessing—quite the opposite of Christians who wait until it's served up on Sunday. But the outcome is the same—life is dispatched with all the consummate skill of an extermination camp. Prayer is no substitute for compassion seldom voiced and thinly held, but it does help alleviate the absurdity of double-think that animal lovers are prone to.

A slaughterhouse can only be thought of as a nightmare by someone who has stopped sleeping. While it exists it is, like these images (the horrific photographs accompanying the article), its own justification, the civilized extension of Man the Hunter, who has an unspoken right to it. After all, he is the apex of creation, isn't he?

One afternoon the child of a fellow student saw these images—to comfort his distress his mother told him they were not real.

BOB LEWIS
An extract from: *Meat Factory: Dispatches from the Killing Floor*
The Beast Summer 1981 No 10

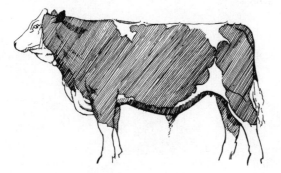

June 24

Two major impulses have motivated, guided and shaped my entire life . . . one of these . . . is an intuitive affinity with the so-called spiritual aspects of life. A deeply-rooted awareness of a quality of 'otherness' which lies behind the physical, ordinary, everyday world in which our gross sensibilities often appear to hold us prisoner.

A natural extension of these deeply-ingrained feelings is my instinctive and unshakeable love affair with all that lives and breathes—nature and her wonderful works. In particular, the animal kingdom. I have held a lifelong fondness of animals, along with a conviction amounting to certainty that nature's children were not put there to be exploited indiscriminately, as raw materials from which we may obtain non-essential luxuries, such as perfumes and cosmetics, or even necessities, in the form of food, clothing and medication. That is why I am a vegetarian and why I fight so hard to prevent the wholesale cruelty to and slaughter of innocent creatures . . .

Since my early childhood, the eating of animals has always been repugnant to me and I am sure that many children feel the same way. Unfortunately, lots of parents are not so understanding as my mother and they and school authorities force such food onto them . . . I think . . . that it is simply a case of conditioning; an unwarranted, ingrained habit of our society—and one which considers itself civilized at that—to accede to the slaughter of millions of our fellow creatures.

THE RT HON MURIEL, THE LADY DOWDING 1908–
Founder of the Beauty Without Cruelty Movement, pioneer vegetarian and anti-vivisectionist campaigner
Beauty—Not The Beast (An autobiography)
Neville Spearman 1980

June 25

Our world is fast approaching crisis point. Each of us has to decide where we stand—to choose between change or no-change. For all practical purposes, it's a decision between life and death or, in more dramatic terms, between good and evil. The battle lines have never before been so clearly drawn, nor so unequally balanced. On the side of no-change are all the tyrants, despots, power-hungry, selfish and short-sighted people of the world, who will resist any challenge to their dominion. Those people (and there are many of them) share a common unspoken philosophy—they believe that humans have no obligations to each other, not to their fellow creatures, not to the planet as a whole. They believe that Might is Right, and that the strongest has licence to exploit the weakest . . .

The act of gathering, preparing and eating food is one of the most fundamental in any form of human society . . . So what happens if we begin to make some pretty basic changes to the way we go about feeding ourselves? . . . On a personal and purely physical level, you should start to feel in better shape. But that's just the beginning . . .

. . . the cynics will tell us . . . the world can't be changed just by one person giving up eating meat . . . But it's the *first step* . . . If we don't take the first step, the alternative is simply to give up the struggle and abandon our world to the darkness that threatens it . . .

The next step is up to you. By changing your own life, you will begin to change the world . . . (but) it's not enough to just kick the flesh food habit . . . you also have a duty to spread the word to other people . . . it all counts, and moves this world one step closer to the next, and more exciting, stage in the human race's history.

PETER COX 1955–
Writer
Why You Don't Need Meat
Bloomsbury Publishing Ltd 1993

June 26

FESTIVAL

This harvest's gathered, sweat is dry;
Before the congregation lie
Pulled crops, whose delicacy taints
By spectral light of window saints.
Praise food on this Thanksgiving Day
Not in a false, divisive way;
Consider kindly all you eat,
Including creatures raised for meat.
Obeisance to these flowers is great
Where stench of beast would desecrate,
And Hawker's sheaves made fairer show
Than butchery at Morwenstow.
Parishioners care not a jot
That hacks and spillage be the lot
Of food beasts. Parish godhead cedes
Predominantly human needs:
In quasi-sacrificial acts
They shoot the bolt and wield the axe.
Their slaughterhouses have high walls,
With priests in bloody overalls.
From fetid confines of this bond
Deliver beasts above, beyond.
All gentle, kind and virtuous men
Would better be for sparing them.

DENNIS JONES MD
Physician
1993

June 27

Mr T'ien, of the State of Ch'i was holding an ancestral banquet in his hall, to which a thousand guests had been invited. As he sat in their midst, many came up to him with presents of fish and game. Eyeing them approvingly, he exclaimed with unction: 'How generous is Heaven to Man! Heaven makes the five kinds of grain to grow, and brings forth the finny and the feathered tribes, especially for our benefit.' All Mr T'ien's guests applauded this sentiment to the echo, except the twelve-year-old son of a Mr Pao who, regardless of seniority, came forward and said: 'It is not as my Lord says. The ten thousand creatures (in the universe) and we ourselves belong to the same category, that of living things, and in this category there is nothing noble and nothing mean. It is only by reason of size, strength, or cunning, that one particular species gains mastery over another, or that one feeds upon another. None is produced in order to subserve the uses of others. Man catches and eats those that are fit for (his) food, but how (could it be maintained that) Heaven produced them just for him? Mosquitoes and gnats suck (blood through) his skin; tigers and wolves devour his flesh—but we do not therefore assert that Heaven produced man for the benefit of mosquitoes and gnats, or to provide food for tigers and wolves.'

Taoist Teachings
From the Book of Lieh Tzu; translated by Richard Wilhelm 1873–1930, missionary and pastor in China, sinologue and theologian

June 28

. . . Flesh eating . . . appears to be by no means a natural taste with the young. Few children like that part of the meal which consists of meat, but prefer the pudding, and fruit, or the vegetables, if well-dressed, which unhappily is not often the case. Many children manifest great repugnance to meat at first, and are coaxed and even scolded by anxious mothers until the habit of eating it is acquired. Adopting the insular creed, which regards beef and mutton as necessary to health, the mother suffers from groundless forebodings about the future of a child who rejects flesh . . . I am satisfied, if the children followed their own instincts in this matter, the result would be a gain in more ways than one. Certainly if meat did not appear in the nursery until the children sent for it, it would rarely be seen there, and the young ones would thrive better on milk and eggs, with the varied produce of the vegetable kingdom.

SIR HENRY THOMPSON FRCS MB 1820–1904

June 29

'Mummy, what is meat and what is fish?'
'It's the dead bodies of animals and fishes.'
'Don't let me ever be given anything like that again.'

Cassian Hall, at four years old, talking to his mother on return from his day at nursery school. Having been allowed to choose when at school, he never ate flesh or fish after that day. (Rebecca Hall)

June 30

To attain, by mutual helpfulness, the realization of the Christ-life, by the path of self-denial, self-sacrifice, and absolute self-abandonment to the Divine Will and Service:

It is these things that the Cross as a symbol speaks. It stands for the sign of the Order of the Cross, because its three steps are those which have to be taken in order to arrive at that Estate which it symbolizes. It speaks of the quest after the humble spirit and the pure heart. It speaks also of that further state of realization when the Soul gives itself in absolute abandonment for the Divine Service. The Three Steps are:

Purity of Living

Purity of Mind

Purity of Soul

Thus to endeavour by example and teaching to win all men to the love of Truth, Purity and Right-doing.

To proclaim the Brotherhood of Man, the essential one-ness of all religious aspirations, and the unity of all living creatures in the Divine.

To teach the moral necessity for humaneness towards all men and all creatures.

To protest against, and to work for, the abolition of, all national and social customs which violate the teachings of the Christ, especially such as involve bloodshed, the oppression of the weak and defenceless, the perpetuation of the brutal mind, and the infliction of cruelty upon animals, viz: war, vivisection, the slaughter of animals for food, fashion and sport and kindred evils.

To advocate the universal adoption of a bloodless diet, and the return to simple, natural foods.

To proclaim a message of peace and happiness, health and purity, spirituality and Divine Love.

REV JOHN TODD FERRIER 1855–1943
Foundation Statement
The Order of the Cross: 10, Devere Gardens, Kensington, London W8

July 1

SHEEP HOOFPRINTS IN LEICESTERSHIRE

These meres run into each other through narrow mouths
Tongues of land stretch over the bright grey water
An early winter's morning—deadly cold
And on the close-cropped slopes that go down
        to all the shores
The prints of sheephoofs
Millions—close as weave in cloth—not one untrodden spot
So that the earth is like a skin patterned
        with sleepers' eyes
In this fenced field the black-shinned black-faced sheep
        walk the world
Where children's tears fall on their naked feet
And if I stretch my hand they gently flinch away
Or touch the earth—it smears it with this clay
And when will you stop sending creatures you call
        symbol of your god
To butchers' hired-hands to stick and flay
And training armies in the night to kill
        the innocence of day?

EDWARD BOND 1934–
British dramatist and poet

July 2

I saw four horses lined up to be killed in sight of each other. A foal stood at the end of the line, trembling in abject terror. The wild brumbies suffer terribly—their first meeting with man is the helicopter that comes to muster them. They then endure many days' journey in intense heat. Australian horsemeat goes to Japan and Belgium. Some even goes to Britain.

Many Australian horses go to Japan. There I saw them stabled in dirty, uncomfortable, intensive conditions for months on end, overfed to the point of sickness, to await not always a humane bullet, but the smash of the primitive poleaxe . . .

Anyone who could send a horse to an end such as I saw could not have an ounce of humanity in them.

CHRIS LARTER
Horse expert and international animal welfare campaigner
Report on the Horse Trade 1981
Chris Larter saw worse sights on subsequent visits to Australian abattoirs. She wrote, 'One hardened British horseman said he had to put down my report four times before he could finish it because he had to keep wiping away the tears.'

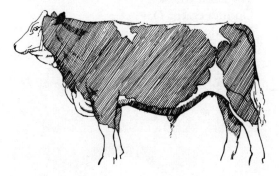

July 3

What have you done?
The Lord will say,
On Judgement Day
On Judgement Day

What have you done
To fur and bone?
What have you done
To my own, to my own?

Slowly, in pain
You made them die,
I heard them cry,
I heard them cry.

Oh, did you not see
The beauty and grace
That you did deface?
That you did deface?

They responded to love,
They responded to life,
But you cut them up
With a knife, with a knife.

What have you done?
The Lord will say,
On Judgement Day
On Judgement Day.

RUTH ALBERT
The Ark August 1986

July 4

'The first time I ever entered a battery house I thought it was the entrance to Hell.'

VIOLET SPALDING
(Co-founder of Chicken's Lib, now Farm Animal Welfare Network) on visiting Lord Nugent's hen battery

☙ ❧

July 5

There was still the inevitable foul stench, the morning pile of rejected dead birds, lorry loads of live chickens waiting for a considerable time by the slaughterhouse, limbs and feathers sticking awkwardly out of crates, dead and dying birds clearly visible from the backs of lorries, rows of birds hung upside down to begin the conveyor belt trip to death, and the sight and noise of the mixer churning up the unwanted feathers.

(Observer at a poultry plant)
Voiceless Victims
REBECCA HALL
Wildwood House 1984

July 6

We are involved in every creature's death,
Our spirits are diminished when they go
To worlds unknown to us beyond the breadth
Of this, where many have endured such woe.

LIAM BROPHY PHD 1910–
Irish poet and essayist; vegetarian and anti-vivisectionist
The Ark (Journal of the Catholic Study Group for Animal Welfare)

July 7

SUN VALLEY

It was the first time they had seen the light,
and gazing, they were too dazed by the sun's
radiance to murmer when their legs were caught

From under them: with a clean snap of bones
as they were lifted out, reminding me
of Yule feasts, or the faint click of a stone's

Fall down a chasm. One, that had dropped free,
was frightened by a ground so fathomless;
its wings flapped and its legs flopped uselessly.

More fathoms to my vision was the place
where they were hung upon the hooks that bore
them swiftly onwards, upside-down in space;

the cause I know not, but all as they hung there
let fall a rain of excrement, whence came
the gross miasma everyone must bear.

How weak are the words, and how unfit to frame
my concept—which lags after what was shown
so far, it flatters it to call it lame!

And it might be ten thousand fowl or one
went smoothly past the imperceptible
electric impulse where they had begun

their afterlife, wings fluttering the while;
and even after they had been thrust through
the cutter, headless they were fluttering still.

But swiftly after that their power to move
compassion vanished—as when journeying far
down through Inferno, one's own power to love

Vanishes like the sun and the other stars.

D M THOMAS 1935–
Novelist, poet and translator from Russian
Dreaming in Bronze Secker & Warburg 1981
The Extended Circle Centaur Press/Cardinal

July 8

. . . They expect to lose 5,000 out of the 30,000 chicks just because of the way they are handled . . .

The stench in these sheds is horrendous. When they are adult, they're so big, so fat, so pumped full of hormones and antibiotics they can't move. It's pitch black. They are always in the dark . . . If you happened to leave the door open, an incredible noise would start up. They get excited at light because they can see each other . . . They are only a day old when they arrive and are killed at three months, or even two.

Hundreds die of suffocation . . . They are craving for warmth and huddle close together, one on top of the other. It is nothing to walk along one of these buildings and pick up twenty or thirty dead chicks . . . Any weak ones have their necks broken . . . I can only say it was like walking into the bowels of Hell.

They all live in Hell, all the time they are alive. And no-one cares.

JENNY GRIDLEY
Animal rights campaigner
A Testimony for Turkeys in *Voiceless Victims* (Rebecca Hall)
Wildwood House 1984

July 9

The better sort here pretend to the utmost compassion for animals of every kind; to hear them speak, a stranger would be apt to imagine they could hardly hurt the gnat that stung them. They seem so tender, and so full of pity, that one would take them for the harmless friends of the whole creation . . . I have seen the very men who have thus boasted of their tenderness, at the same time devour the flesh of six different animals, tossed up in a fricassee. Strange contrariety of conduct. They pity, and they eat the objects of their compassion . . .

O ye simple, honest Brahmins of the East! Ye inoffensive friends of all that were born to happiness as well as you! You never sought a short-lived pleasure from the miseries of other creatures!

. . . You never surfeited upon a guilty meal! How much more purified and refined are all your sensations than ours!

OLIVER GOLDSMITH 1728–1774
Irish-born English poet, playwright and novelist
Letter to the Public Ledger Number XV

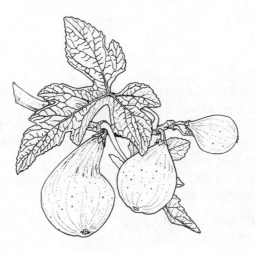

July 10

They turn to-night and freely share
Whate'er my cell bestows,
My rushy couch and frugal fare,
My blessing and repose.

No flocks that range the valley free,
To slaughter I condemn;
Taught by the power that pities me,
I learn to pity them.

But from the mountain's grassy side,
A guiltless feast I bring,
A scrip with herbs and fruit supplied
And water from the spring.

Then, pilgrim, turn, thy cares forego,
All earth-born cares are wrong;
Man wants but little here below,
Nor wants that little long.

OLIVER GOLDSMITH   1728–1774
The Hermit

∾ ∾

July 11

During August-October 1987 nearly 80,000 square miles of Brazilian forest were deliberately devastated by fire, representing 4% of the entire Amazonian region. According to the 'New York Times' *cattle ranchers are responsible for 80% of the destruction* of the carbon-dioxide absorbing forest cover. In 1988, 518 million tonnes of carbonic gasses were produced by Amazon fires—a fifth of the world total, along with large quantities of ozone-depleting oxides.

Environmental Digest No 17, Oct 1988

July 12

(We) will be contradicted in all those camps where people still cling to the opinion that meat-eating is good and necessary for mankind, and believe that a meatless diet is not satisfying. Although this point of view and this belief are supported neither by science nor by experience, they are none the less passionately maintained. It is this attitude which hampers the recovery of civilized humanity and creates manifold confusion. But when we consider how 'all too human' man's nature is, it is an understandable attitude. Meat is not only a food (albeit a defective one), but also a strong stimulant, which is even capable of exciting in the body conditions similar to a kind of intoxication; therefore man's attitude towards it resembles his attitude towards alcoholic drinks.

M BIRCHER-BENNER MD 1867–1939
Children's Diet
C W Daniel & Co Ltd 1946

July 13

A Bengali poem by Swami Vivekananda, a prophet of the New India, says that serving a Jiva (living being) is the greatest form of worship. Service must not remain confined to the human species; it must embrace subhuman creatures as well. Thomas à Kempis says in the Imitation of Christ that there is no creature so little and so worthless as not to manifest goodness in its life.

. . . If one is sincere, and keeps in mind the ideal of eliminating every form of avoidable and unnecessary cruelty and killing, one's compassion and discretion shows the right path of non-violence to follow . . . there cannot be a true civilization without pity and compassion, and such a civilization must advocate humane food, humane dress, humane spirit, humane medicaments and humane pursuits . . .

To be moral, we must not have food by cruelty or killing; morality demands that we must be vegetarians . . . The prevailing morality and law do not allow us to be cannibals. In the future, when there will be an extension of morality and law, society will not allow us to be meat-eaters.

SWAMI AVYAKTANANDA 1901–1990
The Liberation of Animals (1970)
Vedanta Movement, Bath

July 14

A Robin Redbreast in a Cage
Puts all Heaven in a Rage.
A dove house fill'd with doves and pigeons
Shudders Hell thro' all its regions.
A dog starved at his Master's gate
Predicts the ruin of the State . . .
A horse misus'd upon the Road
Calls to Heaven for Human blood.
Each outcry of the hunted Hare
A fibre from the Brain does tear.
A skylark wounded in the wing,
A cherubim does cease to sing . . .
The Lamb misus'd breeds Public strife
And yet forgives the Butcher's knife . . .
He who shall hurt the little Wren
Shall never be belov'd by Men.
He who the ox to wrath has mov'd
Shall never be by Woman lov'd.
The wanton Boy that kills the fly
Shall feel the Spider's enmity . . .
Kill not the Moth nor Butterfly,
For the Last Judgement draweth nigh.

WILLIAM BLAKE 1757–1827
English poet, painter and mystic
From *Auguries of Innocence*

July 15

CHARGE OF A LIE
(Sun Valley— poultry farms and factory)

Half a mile, half a mile
Half a mile onward,
Into the Valley of Death
Ride the seven times six hundred.
Out of the stinking shed.
'Crush them into the lorry!' he said:
On into the Valley of Death
Rode the seven times six hundred.

'Out of the stinking shed!'
They didn't know they'd soon be dead
No, not a single bird knew
'Profit' the board of directors had thundered:
Theirs not to make reply,
Theirs not to reason why,
Theirs to be born and die:
Into the Valley of Death
Rode the seven times six hundred.

Shouting to the right of them,
Swearing to the left of them,
Stranglehold in front of them,
Ignorance blundered
Crushed into crates pell-mell,
Stoically they rode and well,
Into the mouth of Hell
Rode the seven times six hundred.

How many humans will care?
Who'll pluck white feathers from the air?
Who'll feel their black despair?
The silent cargo trundled on while
Hardly a human wondered
At compassion's death, no token
For the wings that are broken;
Anguish and pain,
So few have spoken
For the battered and sundered.

(continued)

July 15   (continued)

There is no return,
Not for the seven times six hundred.

Knives to the left of them,
Scalding baths to the right of them,
Hooks behind them:
Men have blundered;
Grabbed at—something to sell,
Throats cut, eyes bloodied as darkness fell,
The life gone they loved as well,
Gone into the jaws of Death,
Into the mouth of Hell,
Dead bodies now left of them,
Left of the seven times six hundred.

When can their glory fade?
The meekness of dying they made!
Few ever wondered
Cry out for the journey they made!
Cry out at the Death Brigade
Remember the seven times six hundred.

REBECCA HALL
Anglican Society for the Welfare of Animals Bulletin No 40 1992

July 16

Cold turkey may be frightening, judging by one analyst's experience last year. He bought a fresh killed turkey which his wife plucked, leaving it in the kitchen before they went out to dinner.

They returned home to find a naked, gobbling turkey anxiously huddled by the stove. It had been stunned rather than slaughtered and the heat had revived it. After some effort they managed to get a jersey onto it, which remained in place until the feathers grew again.

It has now become a family pet.

The Jewish Vegetarian
March 1991

∽ ∾

July 17

From our experience in testing electrical low-voltage hand stunners on domestic fowls, turkeys and ducks, it does appear that some of the manufacturers, most of the users, and probably some of the inspecting officers are not really aware of the differences between electrical paralysis and electrical narcosis (state of sensibility).

N N SCOTT MRCVS
UFAW Symposium (Universities Federation For Animal Welfare UK)

∽ ∾

July 18

In chicken plants the electrical stunning baths cannot cope with birds in a state of panic, flapping their wings, their heads swinging about. They tend not to make good contact with the stunning machine, and therefore either come out of it unstunned or regain consciousness before their throats are cut. The staff at packaging points have even complained on occasion that the birds are still apparently alive after they have been through the scalding tank and then through the defeathering machine.

DAVID WHITING
Formerly Fieldworker for Beauty Without Cruelty, the World Society For The Protection of Animals, and Compassion in World Farming

July 19

The following pages were written in the Concentration Camp in Dachau, in the midst of all kinds of cruelties. They were furtively scrawled in a hospital barrack where I stayed during my illness, in a time when Death grasped day by day after us, when we lost twelve thousand within four and a half months . . .

You asked me why I do not eat meat and you are wondering at the reasons of my behaviour . . . I refuse to eat animals because I cannot nourish myself by the sufferings and by the death of other Creatures. I refuse to do so, because I suffered so painfully myself that I can feel the pains of others by recalling my own sufferings . . .

I am not preaching . . . I am writing this letter to you, to an already awakened individual who rationally controls his impulses, who feels responsible, internally and externally, for his acts, who knows that our supreme court is sitting in our conscience . . .

I have not the intention to point out with my finger . . . I think it is much more my duty to stir up my own conscience . . .

That is the point: I want to grow up in a better world where a higher law grants more happiness, in a new world where God's commandment reigns: *You shall love each other.*

EDGAR KUPFER
Animals My Brethren
An Essay which came out of Dachau in April 1945; now in a Special Collection Library of the University of Chicago

July 20

(Porphyry) regards other animals as our brothers, because they are endowed with life as we are, because they have the same principles of life, the same feelings, the same ideas, memory, industry—as we. (Human) speech alone is wanting in them. If they had it should we dare to kill and eat them? Should we dare to commit these fratricides?

FRANÇOIS VOLTAIRE 1694–1778
French satirist, philosopher, historian, dramatist and poet
Viande

July 21

I was returning home and took the garden path. My dog walked in front of me. Suddenly he stood still, then began to crawl as though he scented game. I looked along the path and saw on the ground a baby sparrow with yellow around his beak and downy fluff upon his head. He had fallen out of the nest (the wind was shaking the branches of the trees along the path). There he lay motionless, his little wings spread out impotently.

My dog approached him slowly, when suddenly, an old sparrow with a black breast tore himself from a nearby tree and fell like a stone in front of his muzzle. Ruffled and terrified he hopped several times with a pitiful cry in front of the gaping jaws then hurled himself in protection of his offspring covering him with his body. Trembling with terror his little voice became wild and hoarse. Paralysed with fear he sacrificed himself. What an enormous monster the dog must have appeared and yet he could not stay in safety on the branch, a power stronger than his will had thrown him down.

My dog Treasure stopped and drew back, one believes he too had sensed a superior power. I quickly called the slightly confused dog and went away full of respect. Do not laugh: I bowed respectfully before the heroic little bird and his impulse of love.

And, I thought, love is stronger than death and the fear of death and it is only by love that life is sustained and its rhythm continues.

IVAN TURGENEV 1818–1883
Russian novelist
The Sparrow (1878)
Translated from French by Ann Caldwell

July 22

Ahimsa in India in the Fifth Century:
The inhabitants are numerous and happy . . . Throughout the country the people *do not kill any living creature*, nor drink intoxicating liquor . . . they do not keep pigs and fowl, and do not sell live cattle; in the markets *there are no butcher shops* and no dealers in intoxicating drink . . . Only the Chandalas (the lowest and most despised caste) are fishermen and hunters and sell flesh meat.

FA-HSIEN
Chinese Buddhist pilgrim to India. 5th Century
Translated by James Legge (A Record of Buddhist Kingdoms)
Ahimsa: non-violence or harmlessness

July 23

On a pilgrimage to India in the 1950's, I marvelled at the same phenomenon of the absence of butcher shops and liquor stores. India is a vegetarian's delight. It is not that the Indians can't afford flesh foods, but that every great spiritual figure in India—including in modern times Mohandas Gandhi—so emphasized non-violence and harmlessness to living beings that even wealthy Indians spurn animal flesh. The unique Indian reverence and gratitude toward the cow, the surrogate mother of the human race, should therefore come as no surprise. While other 'civilized' nations butcher the docile cow when she can no longer give them milk, Indians protect her by according her the status of sacred. It is to the everlasting credit of Gandhi that even in the face of much opposition he resolutely defended the protection of cows.

ROSHI PHILIP KAPLEAU 1912–
Buddhist Monk and American Zen Master
A Buddhist Case for Vegetarianism
Rider & Co. 1983

July 24

Swami Sri Shantipuriji had a mystical experience after the death of his wife and went to live in the jungle, taking up the life of an ascetic, living upon wild roots.

Krishnanand of the Shanti Ashram Bhadram in Bangalore went to visit the holy man:

We got up and proceeded to the place where he was. By the time we reached near him, he had sat down and by his side we saw a big long python. On seeing us, he stood up and welcomed us in an intimate manner. Asking us not to bother about the python, he said: 'I am glad you have come.' Then motioning us to sit down, he himself sat at the very place where he had stood and drew the python well close to him . . . The python coiled itself and lay motionless.

. . . The silent saint rose . . . and ran past us, leaving the python to lie where it was. All of us turned back to see. Lo, we saw a lioness with two cubs. The running saint signalled to them with downward waves of his hands, to sit down. The queen of the forest meekly obeyed—sprawling itself on the ground and the playful cubs lingered by. As he neared them, Shantipuriji slowed down and quickly sat before the lioness hiding its facial view from us. Then, by his right hand he grabbed one of the cubs and pressed it close to his side and by the other he was stroking the head of the lioness. In the meanwhile, the other cub stole from behind and stood up holding by its forelegs the left shoulder of the saint . . .

Shri Shantipuriji rose and muttered something to the massive beast . . . Perhaps he said, 'You see, good lady, I have guests.' . . . The lioness picked up its weighty body understandingly, looked in our direction and sprinted off with the parting pat from its saintly friend.

We weren't further than thirty feet from the spot where the scene of beastly ferociousness bowing to 'TRUE LOVE' was enacted. We were exhilarated beyond measure. The effects of TRUE LOVE are magical indeed. Because we lack much in TRUE LOVE, we confront the bad effects of hatred, jealousy, mistrust, attacks and wars.

REV SWAMI KRISHNANAND 1920–1989
Light and Darkness
Shanti Ashram 1969

July 25

I do not regard flesh food as necessary for us. I hold flesh food to be unsuited to our species. We err in copying the lower animal world if we are superior to it . . .

The only way to live is to let live.

MOHANDAS GANDHI 1869–1948

July 26

We might as well eat the flesh of men as the flesh of other animals.

DIOGENES 400-325 BC
Greek philosopher

July 27

How shocked and self-righteous we become when we learn that cannibalism still exists in . . . Africa, Australia, Polynesia, and South America, but to what degree are we superior? We make wars, kill and eat animal flesh; then in our smug self-approval we seek the blessing of our Creator; . . . so does the cannibal—but he is less hypocritical. . .

Some interesting sidelights into the cannibal mind are given in Volbard's *Cannabilism*.

'There is no difference—meat is meat. Everything that has life is the same. It's food to eat.'

'Meat is meat' is a favourite self-justification when confronted with the white man's accusations. It is a matter of where you draw the line, whether as a society or as an individual.

'I do not interfere when you kill a goat—why do you interfere when I kill a slave?'

'You eat animals of a low order, whereas we eat man, the most noble of animals. Therefore you are degenerate, not we.'

Another cannibal reply to European indignation is rather the same as that given by white carnivores to their fellow vegetarians:

'This is our tradition. Our fathers and forefathers have always done so, and we must continue . . .' Also, 'Yes, we do eat man-flesh—but only a *little* . . .'

In 'civilized' society if an individual does not eat a particular food . . . due to personal dislike, no one pays overmuch attention . . . and certainly no one worries for his survival. But should one . . . claim not to eat animal flesh, then the carnivore's reaction is extreme . . .

Like the carnivore, (the cannibal) immediately becomes suspicious. When it is suggested to him that one can live without this form of nourishment, he goes on the defensive and shows all the signs of mental stress . . . shown by a drug addict when threatened with withdrawal . . . or the average European carnivore threatened with withdrawal of animal flesh . . . scholars agree that human flesh, animal flesh and drugs show the same tendency to addiction . . .

VIVIEN PICK
Doctor of Music, third generation vegetarian and the originator of the Jewish Vegetarian Society
Cannibals and Carnivores from *Tree of Life*
(An anthology from the *Jewish Vegetarian* 1966–1974, edited by Philip L Pick)
A S Barnes & Co. NJ, USA 1977

July 28

The cannibal goes out and hunts, pursues and kills another man and proceeds to cook and eat him precisely as he would any other game. There is not a single argument nor a single fact that can be offered in favour of flesh eating that cannot be offered, with equal strength, in favour of cannibalism.

DR HERBERT SHELTON 1895–
American naturopathic physician
Superior Nutrition

☙ ☞

July 29

Dennis Weaver scorns coffee, and for almost thirty years has been a teetotaling vegetarian—a fact that used to stun his fans at the barbecues and dinner parties that were held in his honour. An actor who played a deputy marshall in the West's most notorious cattle town was expected to eat beef and gulp liquor like a cowboy . . .

He also starred in a series that ran for nearly three years. In 'Gentle Ben', he played a game warden who kept a seven hundred pound black bear as a pet. This time, Weaver was side-kick to a bear instead of Marshall Dillon of 'Gunsmoke'. Of Ben, Weaver recalls, 'Our bear was a vegetarian. There was a scene in which he was supposed to devour a hotdog, and he wouldn't have any part of it. In order to give the illusion that he was eating hotdogs, we had to make them out of a vegetarian product; as soon as we did, he gobbled them right up.'

DENNIS WEAVER 1924–
American actor; star of 'McCloud'
Famous Vegetarians and Their Favorite Recipes
by Rynn Berry, 'the Boswell of Vegetarianism'.
Panjandrum Books 1990. Distrib. Talman & Co. Inc. NY USA & Centaur Press UK

July 30

In all the round world of Utopia there is no meat. There used to be. But now we cannot stand the thought of the slaughterhouse. And in a population that is all educated and at about the same level of physical refinement, it is practically impossible to find anyone who will hew a dead ox or pig. We never settled the hygienic aspect of meat-eating at all. This other aspect decided us. I can still remember as a boy the rejoicings over the closing of the last slaughterhouse.

H G WELLS 1866–1946
English novelist and journalist, known for his science fiction, satirical novels and popularized accounts of history and science
A Modern Utopia

꩜ ꩜

July 31

You take a beautiful girl down to supper and you offer her—a ham sandwich! It is proverbial folly to cast pearls before swine. What are we to say of the politeness which casts swine before pearls?

HENRY SALT 1851–1939
English writer, humanitarian and social reformer
The Humanities of Diet
The Humanitarian League 1897

August 1

Since compassion for animals is so intimately associated with goodness of character, it may be confidently asserted that whoever is cruel to animals cannot be good to man.

ARTHUR SCHOPENHAUER 1788–1860
German philosopher

~ ~

August 2

You have just dined; and however scrupulously the slaughterhouse is concealed in a graceful distance of miles, there is complicity.

RALPH WALDO EMERSON 1803–1883
American essayist, philosopher and poet

~ ~

August 3

Were the belief to become one day general that man could dispense with animal food, there would ensue not only a great economic revolution . . . but a moral improvement as well.

COUNT MAURICE MAETERLINK 1862–1949
Belgian playwright, essayist and poet
The Buried Temple

August 4

Oh, Ox, how great are thy desserts! A being without guile, harmless, simple, willing for work! Ungrateful and unworthy of the fruits of earth, man his own farm labourer slays and smites with the axe that toil-worn neck that had so oft renewed for him the face of the hard earth; so many harvests given!

OVID 43 BC–17 AD
Roman poet

∾ ∾

August 5

Thus, no creature ever
comes short of its own completeness.
Wherever it stands,
it does not fail to cover the ground.

ZEN MASTER DOGEN

August 6

In order to maximize milk production goats undergo carefully planned pregnancies in much the same way as dairy cows. Most of the males that are born are either slaughtered at birth or fattened up for a few months to be killed for meat. 50,000 male goat kids are slaughtered every year in this country because they are economically useless. They are chloroformed or have their necks broken—there is no precise legislation. The welfare code only states that they should be 'humanely killed'!

Many kids are either exported to the Middle East or (increasingly) killed here by 'ritual' slaughter methods, ie killing the animals without first pre-stunning them so they are fully conscious when they die. The meat is required for religious reasons by Jewish and Moslem communities.

AMANDA ROFE 1962–
Campaigner for animal liberation
The Vegan, Spring 1990

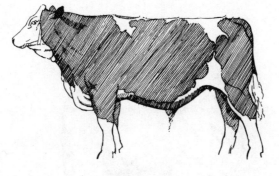

August 7

Meat can never be obtained without injuring creatures, and injury to sentient beings is detrimental to heavenly bliss; therefore, one should shun meat eating . . .

One should consider the disgusting origin of flesh and the cruelty of fettering and slaying corporeal beings, and entirely abstain from flesh eating . . .

He who permits the slaughter of animals, he who cuts up, kills, buys, sells, cooks, serves it up and eats—every one of these is a slayer of animals . . .

He who seeks to increase his own flesh with the flesh of others, not worshipping the gods or manes, is the greatest of all sinners . . .

Meat cannot be obtained from straw or stone. It can be obtained only by slaughtering a creature, hence meat is not to be eaten . . .

Others should be treated as one's own Self and should be protected as such.

KOSHELYA WALLI
The Conception of Ahimsa in Indian Thought   (from Hindu Scriptures)
Battacharya, Varanasi, India   1974

August 8

Chinese monks who abstained from meat were able to perform rites for the dead with greater effectiveness. If lay people knew that meat was being eaten at a monastery, it was less likely to receive their patronage . . . This accounts for the complaints by foreign travellers in China that monks would not allow them even to pass the night at their temples because of the fear that meat might be smuggled in and eaten on the premises.

HOLMES WELCH
The Practice of Chinese Buddhism 1900–1950
Boston, Harvard University Press 1967

❧ ❧

August 9

In China and Japan the eating of meat was looked upon as an evil and was ostracized . . . The eating of meat gradually ceased (around 517) and this tended to become general. It became a matter of course not to use any kind of meat in the meals of temples and monasteries.

Encyclopaedia of Buddhism (Edited by G P Malasekera)
Government of Ceylon Press 1963

August 10

In eating flesh, and thereby ingesting the blood principle—*flesh and blood being inseparable*—man sacrifices to the astral emanations of his own magnetic atmospheres and so doing, ministers to the terrene and corruptible. Thus it is to 'eat the tongue offered to idols,' for blood is the food of the astral Eidola and the eater of blood is infested by them . . . let us say boldly, and without fear of contradiction from those who really *know*, that the Interior life and the clear Heaven are not attainable by men who are partakers of blood: men whose mental atmosphere is thick with the crimes of daily sacrifices to idols. For so long as these shadows infest the Man, obscuring the expanse of the higher and divine Ether beyond, he remains unable to detach himself from the love for Matter and from the attractions of Sense, and can at best but dimly discern the Light of the Spiritual form . . .

Abstinence from bloody oblations on all planes is therefore the gate of the Perfect Way, the test of illumination, the touchstone and criterion of sincere desire for the fulness of Beatific Vision.

ANNA KINGSFORD 1846–1898
The Perfect Way, or *The Finding of Christ*
Field & Iver & Hamilton Adams & Co 1882 Scribner NY USA

August 11

The Lord will abhor both the bloodthirsty and deceitful man . . . Their inward parts are very wickedness. Their throat is an open sepulchre.

Psalms v.6.9.
Psalms: The 19th Book of the Old Testament of the Bible, containing 150 hymns, or songs to God. Many are ascribed to David.

August 12

[Berlin 15th July 1908]

The extraordinary credulity which still prevails among a large section of the population was well illustrated today by a prosecution at Brunswick, which resulted in a man named Charles Albrecht being sentenced to three years penal servitude for criminal quackery.

Albrecht practised as a quack doctor at Kirchbruk, and to his many clients he recommended the blood of executed murderers as a remedy for all kinds of ailments.

The demand for this gruesome medicine was enormous, and in order to cope with it, Albrecht obtained a quantity of pig's blood, which he bottled and sold as the blood of beheaded murderers at 12s a bottle. His profits were very large, and his patients, who numbered hundreds, blindly obeying his directions, drank the pig's blood, believing it to be the blood of criminals who had died on the scaffold. The same remedy was recommended for heart disease, consumption, gout, skin diseases, and practically every other form of sickness.

It will be noticed that the only crime supposed to have been committed—and for which punishment was meted out—was the mere imposture by Albrecht of selling some pig's blood for the blood of executed murderers, and so obtaining money by a false pretence for fraud: and the moral condition of the dupes of the quack doctor—who numbered hundreds—who were prepared to drink the blood of executed murderers in order to cure their physical ailments—and this is a Christian country—is described merely as a good illustration of 'extraordinary credulity.'

Daily Express 16th July 1908

August 13

I'm often asked why I became vegetarian. The question invariably arises when I am required to share a table with non-vegetarians, a situation which I would rather avoid, but find it difficult to do so. After twenty two years of experience, I have found it best to preface all my remarks with 'OK I'm happy to discuss this, but you must realize that there is no criticism of you in what I believe or have to say, it's just the way it is for me.' I have found that this is the only way to avoid the conversation deteriorating into an hour of the meat-eaters attempting to justify the unjustifiable. With the element of righteousness removed, the conversation is more spacious, and remarkably, quite a few people have been 'converted' in this way. It is necessary to adopt this approach because I feel the practice of meat-eating is intrinsically neurotic, and those who indulge in it are in a state of deep and irrational denial. I have yet to discover the meat-eater who says 'Yes I know I'm killing, yes it's unhealthy, but I don't care, I like it and I'll continue doing it.' There is always the unmistakable whiff of irrationality, of fear, of anger, or even sadness in their explanations, and they often end with 'well I admire you, but I couldn't do it.' That our whole society is neurotic in this way serves to disguise the plight of the individual who is so threatened by the simple truth that if it is possible to live well and be healthy without killing, then the only justification for killing an animal would be to enjoy the taste of its flesh. This is a proposition so preposterous that we have created monstrous lies to protect ourselves from the realization of our neurosis: that it is important nutritionally to eat meat; that animals do not know fear, love, loss, or pain; that it is economically vital to support the meat industry, and perhaps most disgusting of all, that we have a religious duty to use the animals over which God gave us dominion. The other hypothesis that invariably arises, is 'What would you do if your life *really* depended on eating meat, say after an air crash, or marooned on an island?' I don't know what I would do, but I pray that I would choose to die in health and dignity.

MARTIN SHAW
British actor
A statement written for this book

August 14

From 1874, when Edward Maitland first met Anna Kingsford, until his death, his voice and his pen were ever active in the cause of humanity, and he ever gave of his best. His heart taught him the inhumanity, and therein the wrong and wickedness of flesh-eating. He was faithful to his intuitions: and 'the generation of the faithful shall be blessed.'

I shall ever remember Edward Maitland as one of the greatest, wisest, most lovable and best of men whom it has been my privilege to know: and applying the words to Anna Kingsford and Edward Maitland respectively, I say, with Anna Kingsford:

'Blessed is the Soul whom the just commemorate before God; for whom the poor, and the orphan and the dumb creature weep.'

SAMUEL HOPGOOD HART
Preface to *Addresses and Essays on Vegetarianism*, by Anna Bonus Kingsford
Edited by S H Hart
Watkins 1912

☙ ❧

August 15

There has been a curse upon humanity for a million years. And every time an innocent creature is needlessly killed that curse is renewed.

While one human being is left suffering, I cannot go on, I cannot go in peace.

While one creature is left suffering, I cannot go on, I cannot go in peace.

SWAMI AVYAKANANDA 1901–1990
Words spoken to a small group of people in Southfields, London in 1980

August 16

I will take no bullock out of the house: nor he-goat out of my fold. For all the beasts of the forest are Mine: and so are the cattle upon a thousand hills. I know all the fowls upon the mountains: and the wild beasts of the field are in My sight. If I be hungry I will not tell thee: for the whole world is Mine, and all that is therein. Thinkest thou that I will eat bull's flesh: and drink the blood of goats? . . . Why dost thou preach My laws, and takest My covenant in thy mouth: Whereas thou hatest to be reformed: and hast cast My words behind thee? . . . And thou thoughtest wickedly, that I am even such a one as thyself . . . O, consider thus, ye that forget God.

Psalms 50: 9-22

∽ ∾

August 17

Is it morally lawful for cultivated and refined persons to impose upon a whole class of the population a disgusting brutalizing and unwholesome occupation, which is scientifically and experimentally demonstrable to be not merely entirely needless, but absolutely inimical to the best interests of the human race?

Butchers are the Pariahs of the Western world; the very name itself of their trade has become a synonym for barbarity, and is used as a term of reproach in speaking of persons notorious for brutality, coarseness, or love of bloodshed. The common explanation, 'What a butcher is So-and-so' in reference to such men, betrays the horror and reprobation with which one instinctively regarded the followers of a trade created and patronized chiefly by the 'refined' classes!

ANNA KINGSFORD MD 1846–1888
Social Considerations—Addresses and Essays on Vegetarianism
John Watkins 1912

August 18

(People who eat meat) are responsible for all the pain that grows out of meat-eating, and which is necessitated by the use of sentient animals as food; not only the horrors of the slaughterhouse, but also the preliminary horrors of the railway traffic, of the steamboat and ship traffic; all the starvation and the thirst and the prolonged misery of fear which these unhappy creatures have to pass through for the gratification of the appetites of man . . . All pain acts as a record against humanity and slackens and retards the whole of human growth.

ANNIE BESANT 1847–1933
One of the founders of the Theosophical Movement. Active in India's Movement for Independence

August 19

Barely three months had passed since Yoineh Meir had become a slaughterer, but the time seemed to stretch endlessly. He felt as though he was immersed in blood and lymph. His ears were beset by the squawking of hens, the crowing of roosters, the gobbling of geese, the lowing of oxen, the mooing and bleating of calves and goats; wings fluttered, claws tapped on the floor. The bodies refused to know any justification or excuse—every body resisted in its own fashion, tried to escape, and seemed to argue with the Creator to its last breath.

ISAAC BASHEVIS SINGER 1904–1992
The Slaughterer
From *The Seance*
Avon Books 1969

August 20

My brethren, we are free! The fruits are glowing
Beneath the stars, and the nightwinds are flowing
O'er the ripe corn, the birds and beasts are dreaming—
Never again may blood of bird or beast
Stain with its venomous stream a human feast,
To the pure skies in accusation steaming.
Avenging poisons shall have ceased
To feed disease and fear and madness;
The dwellers of the earth and air
Shall throng around our steps in gladness,
Seeking their food or refuge there.
Our toil from thought all glorious forms shall cull,
To make this Earth, our home, more beautiful;
And Science, and her sister, Poesy,
Shall clothe in light the fields and cities of the Free!

PERCY BYSSHE SHELLEY   1792–1822
English poet
The Revolt of Islam. Canto V

August 21

(The wise of old) were not abstainers of flesh-food by accident, caprice or custom. They were grave, studious, earnest men, of vast knowledge, understanding, and faculty, who deliberately adopted this regimen in pursuance of that which they regarded as the supreme object of an ambition of rational beings. This object, they held, is to turn existence to the best possible account in the long run. This, they held, involved the making of ourselves the best that we have it in us to be. And this, again, they held, can be done only by developing to the utmost all the higher faculties and capacities of our nature.

It was in pursuance of these ends that the wise of old . . . insisted on the (vegetarian) diet, . . . the diet which all seekers after perfection have followed, and the principle of which is that which alone is consistent with perfection, namely, Purity. The first step towards perfection is to build up one's organism of the purest and most suitable materials. And so perfect is the harmony of nature, that that which is best for man on one plane of his system is best for him on all planes. This is to say, that whatever diet best ministers to the health and strength of his physical part, best ministers to those of his intellectual, his moral, and his spiritual part.

EDWARD MAITLAND MA 1824–1907
Lecture

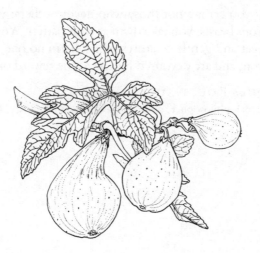

August 22

I am always struck with the idea that all the highest, the purest, the subtlest, the most deep-reaching philosophy which the world holds has come to us from the vegetarian races . . . I think that as long as men live upon the food of the tiger they will have the tiger's nature; but if they adopt the food of the Golden Age—the food of Eden, I care not which you call it,—they will have the nature of Paradise. If the world is to be redeemed we must get back to that beautiful time which is celebrated by all the poets; which haunts evermore the dreams of seers.

ANNA KINGSFORD 1846–1888
Lecture on Historical Aspect of Food Reform
The Food Reform Magazine No 1 July/Sept 1885

∽ ∾

August 23

The animals you eat are not those who devour others; you do not eat the carnivorous beasts, you take them as your pattern. You only hunger after the sweet and gentle creatures which harm no one, which follow you, serve you, and are devoured by you as the reward of their service.

JEAN JACQUES ROUSSEAU 1712–1788
Swiss born French philosopher, political theorist and composer; father of French romanticism
Emile

August 24

THE LAMB

Little Lamb, who made thee?
Dost thou know who made thee?
Gave thee life, and bid thee feed
By the stream and o'er the mead;
Gave thee clothing, wooly, bright;
Gave thee such a tender voice,
Making all the vales rejoice?

Little Lamb, who made thee?
Dost thou know who made thee?
Little Lamb, I'll tell thee,
Little Lamb, I'll tell thee:

He is called by thy name,
For he calls himself a Lamb.
He is meek, and he is mild;
He became a little child.
I a child, and thou a lamb,
We are called by his name.

Little Lamb, God bless thee!
Little Lamb, God bless thee!

WILLIAM BLAKE   1757–1827

August 25

The mystical interpretation of scripture was quite usual in the early church, and Origen says that 'while every passage of scripture has a spiritual meaning, many passages have no other meaning but that there is often a spiritual meaning under a literal fiction.' And Athanasius warns us that 'were we to understand sacred writ according to the letter, we should fall into the most enormous blasphemies as by ascribing cruelty and falsehood to the Deity.'

This is precisely what the non-mystical interpretation of the Gospels has done, for it asks us to believe that the Master, who came to preach a Gospel of love, was so inconsistent in this life that He ate the Creatures and encouraged others to do same. To which the convinced vegetarian can only answer that if the Gospels teach such things then the sooner people stop taking them literally the better.

REV V A HOLMES-GORE
Was the Master a Vegetarian?
Leaflet published by the Vegetarian Society

August 26

Many of the early Christian fathers not only practised and advocated vegetarianism on aesthetic and spiritual grounds but were extremely outspoken to their fellow Christians who hankered after the flesh-pots. This is what Tertullian had to say— 'How unworthily do you press the example of Christ as having come eating and drinking *into the service of your hosts!* I think that He who pronounced not the full but the hungry and thirsty 'Blessed', who professed His work to be the completion of His father's Will, I think that He was wont to abstain, instructing them to labour for that 'meat' which lasts to eternal life, and enjoining in their common prayers petition, not for rich and gross food, but for bread only.

GEOFFREY L RUDD   1909-
The Bible and Vegetarianism
Vegetarian Society

August 27

Man is not and never could have been a carnivore:

Flesh eaters:

1. Have very short bowels for the rapid expulsion of putrefactive bacteria—inseparable from decomposing flesh.
2. Have long teeth and most have retractable claws for killing and holding living prey. Man can only catch and kill the meat-bearing animals with instruments.
3. Have jaws which open only in an up and down motion.
4. Do not sweat through the skin but control body heat by extruding the tongue and by rapid breathing.
5. Their saliva is minus ptyalin and cannot pre-digest starches.
6. They secrete ten times more hydrochloric acid than vegetarians, sufficient to dissolve bones in the diet.
7. They lap water like a cat.

Vegetarians:

1. Have long bowels for dealing with fermentative bacteria, which is evolved in the digestion of vegetarian foods.
2. Do not have sabre-like teeth and claws, though some may have defensive horns.
3. Have jaws which can move sideways for chewing.
4. Have the ferment ptyalin in the saliva for the pre-digestion of starches.
5. Have sweat pores for heat control and the elimination of impurities.
6. Take liquids by suction through the teeth.

Compiled by T H HUXLEY 1825–1895
English biologist

August 28

No physiologist would dispute with those who maintain that man ought to have a vegetable diet.

DR SPENCER THOMPSON
Physiologist

August 29

Orthodox Jews make a blessing for practically all benefits in life. There is a separate blessing for each type of food, but there is none for flesh foods—something that has been slaughtered cannot be blessed. There is a blessing on wearing new garments, but no blessings may be made over furs or other animal skins of any kind—you cannot destroy the works of Creation and at the same time bless God for having made them . . . On Pentecost, when the Synagogues are decorated with fruits and flowers, no carcasses of slaughtered creatures are to be seen. On Succot, when the little booths are erected, they are decorated with fruit and flowers, no bodies nor portions' of bodies are used as decorations . . . On the solemn Day of Atonement, when all Jews fast and seek compassion from the Almighty for life and health in the coming year, no leather shoes should be worn in the Synagogue. The reason for this is not humility, but to avoid hypocrisy. It is not devout to pray for compassion when one has shown no compassion in daily life.

PHILIP L PICK 1910–1992
The Source of our Inspiration
The Jewish Vegetarian Society

August 30

And God said, Behold, I have given you every herb bearing seed, which is upon the face of all the earth, and every tree, in which is the fruit of a tree yielding seed; to you it shall be for meat.

And to every beast of the earth, and to every fowl of the air, and to every thing that creepeth upon the earth, wherein there is life, I have given every green herb for meat; and it was so.

Genesis 1:29,30
First book of the Old Testament: Greek origin
(Hebrew 'Bereshith'—'In the beginning')

⌘ ⌘

August 31

Most people accept the position of eating meat only on condition that the animal has pleasure in life while it lives and is then humanely slaughtered. In no instance can these two criteria be guaranteed today. Many people have become so repulsed by the situation that they have taken the first step towards opting out of it by becoming vegetarians. I use the phrase 'first step' because much suffering is involved in the supply of dairy produce. The vegan, who attempts to eschew all animal products and by-products, takes the most logical step towards elimination of cruelty, a step to which only a very small but gallant minority have so far devoted their lives.

RUTH HARRISON 1920–
Animal Welfare Campaigner, government committee member for farm animal welfare
Animal Machines
Stuart 1964

September 1

It is strange to hear people talk of Humanitarianism, who are members of societies for the prevention of cruelty to children and animals, and who claim to be God-loving men and women, but who, nevertheless, encourage by their patronage the killing of animals merely to gratify the cravings of appetite.

OTOMAN ZAR—ADUSHT HA'NISH MD DD 1844–1936
Mazdaznan Science of Deitetics
Ancient Persian theology

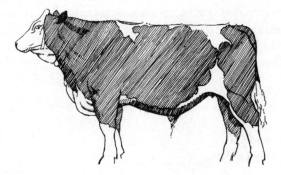

September 2

We who are vegetarians want our dogs and cats to share our clean, healthful, non-cruel daily food . . . Because I am a vegetarian many of my dogs shared the diet and kept very well on it. They seemed to become more gentle and had friendships with my tamed wild birds and many kinds of wild animals . . . All animals require a raw food diet in order to attain total health and a full life span . . . The lives of cats and dogs are short, an average of fourteen years, though I have seen dogs over twenty years of age. All those long livers had been raised on a meatless diet, not because their owners were vegetarians, but because such a diet had been more convenient. One small terrier I saw in Spain, and which was then twenty-three years old, had been raised largely on a diet of goat's milk, boiled and raw onions, and *migas* (lightly boiled wheaten flour with a little oil stirred in when cool) . . .

We know that the old-fashioned diet of the hill shepherd's sheep-herding collies—tireless and mentally alert workers—were mainly oatmeal scalded with salted water—fed out on the hills and moors . . . I have seen dogs eating from garden and field such vegetables and plants as parsley, watercress, mint, brussels sprouts, cabbage stumps, onion tops, wild watercress, garlic, mosses, seaweeds and, of course, their favourite medicinal herb, couch-grass. Dogs also help themselves to many kinds of berries . . . Cats also steal melons, marrows, pumpkins and cucumber.

JULIETTE DE BAIRACLI LEVY
Pioneer in herbal medicine, renowned breeder of Afghan hounds, traveller and author
Healthy Dogs and Cats
Vegetarian Society Leaflet

September 3

In the days when St Francis abode in the city of Gubbio, a huge wolf, terrible and fierce, appeared in the neighbourhood, and not only devoured animals but men also; in such wise that all the citizens went in great fear of their lives, . . . Wherefore St Francis had great compassion for the men of that city . . . he, making the sign of the holy cross, and putting all his trust in God, set forth with his companions; but they, fearing to go further, St Francis went his way alone towards the place where the wolf was. And lo! the said wolf, in the sight of such folk . . . leapt towards St Francis with gaping jaws; and St Francis, drawing nigh, made to him, the sign of the most holy cross and called him, speaking thus, 'Come hither, Friar wolf; I command thee in the name of Christ that thou do hurt neither to me nor to any man.' . . . No sooner was the command uttered than he came, gentle as a lamb, and laid himself at the feet of St Francis . . . Then St Francis speaks to him thus, 'Friar wolf, thou . . . hast wrought grievous ill, destroying and slaying God's creatures without His leave; and . . . thou hast dared to slay men . . . But, Friar wolf, Fain would I make peace with them and thee . . . I promise to obtain for thee, so long as thou livest, a continual sustenance from the men of this city, so that thou shalt no more suffer hunger, for well I ween that thou hast wrought all this evil to satisfy thy hunger . . . I desire that thou promise me to do hurt neither to man nor beast . . . that thou pledge thy faith to me to keep this promise, that I may have full trust in thee.' And . . . the wolf lifted up his right paw and gently laid it in the hand of St Francis . . . Then said St Francis, 'Friar wolf, I command thee in the name of Jesus Christ to come with me; fear nought, and we will go and confirm this peace in the name of God.' And the wolf, obedient, set forth by his side ever as a pet lamb . . . And the said wolf lived two years in Gubbio, and was wont to enter like a tame creature into the houses from door to door . . . he was kindly fed by the people; and as he went about the city never a dog barked at him. At last, after two years, Friar wolf died of old age; whereat the citizens grieved much . . .

FIORETTI c. 1322
(from the Latin)
The Little Flowers of St Francis

September 4

We must never permit the voice of humanity within us to be silenced. It is man's sympathy with all creatures that first makes him truly a man.

ALBERT SCHWEIZER 1875–1965
Philosopher, musician, theologian and medicinal missionary from Alsace, France
Winner of the Nobel Peace Prize in 1952
The Animal World of Albert Schweizer
Bean Press 1951

❧ ❧

September 5

There is so little looking into the essence of things. So little looking at things as they are, and so much thinking and doing as we are accustomed or told to think and do—there are, in fact, so few who can really think at all—that if we had been accustomed and taught to do so from childhood, and the world were practically unanimous in its conduct and teachings on the matter, very few of us indeed would not sit down to a breakfast of scrambled infant's brains, a luncheon of cold boiled aunt, or a dinner of roast uncle, with as little compunction, perhaps with the same horrible merriment, as we today attend a 'barbecue' or a 'turkey'. Why should we not make hash and sausages out of our broken-down grand-fathers and grand-mothers just as we do out of our worn-out horses, and help out the pigeons at our killing carnivals with a few live peasants? How much more artistic and civilized to pile our tables on holy days with the gold and crimson of the fields and orchards than to load them with the dead! And yet how strangely few are mature enough to care anything at all about the matter!

J HOWARD MOORE 1862–1916
American instructor in Zoology
The Universal Kinship (1906 USA)
(Reissue: Ed. by Charles Magel. Centaur Press 1992)

September 6

Wars and concentration camps exist for several years and may be followed by some decades of peace. But the atrocities against animals, as hideous as the worst committed on battlefields and in concentration camps, are being committed incessantly. We can do little to improve the conduct of humans toward their fellow humans if we do not radically change our conduct toward defenceless animals and fight the main cause of animal persecution and torture—meat-eating.

MAGNUS SCHWANTJE 1877–1959
Reverence for Life, Brotherhood and Vegetarianism

September 7

It is in the battery shed where we find the parallel with Auschwitz . . . To shut your mind, heart and imagination from the sufferings of others is to begin slowly, but inexorably, to die. Those Christians who close their minds and hearts to the cause of animal welfare, and the evils it seeks to combat, are ignoring the Fundamental spiritual teachings of Christ himself.

THE RIGHT REVEREND JOHN AUSTIN BAKER 1928–
Bishop of Salisbury
Sermon at York Minster 29.9.86, World Day of Prayer for Animals.

September 8

Flesh foods stimulate the passions, and more, acting as a stimulant in the body, they call for other stimulants to feed and satisfy the appetites thus aroused . . .

The time will come in the world's history, and a movement is setting in that direction even now, when it will be deemed as strange a thing to find a man or a woman who eats flesh as food, as it is now to find (one) who refrains from eating it. . . . I share the belief with many others, that the *highest* mental, physical, and spiritual excellence will come to a person only when, among other things, he refrains from a flesh and blood diet.

RALPH WALDO TRINE
Every Living Creature or Heart-Training Through the Animal World
Thomas Y Crowell & Co NY USA 1899

~ ~

September 9

In Western society, modern industrial man demands an ever-higher standard of living. The improvements he demands are not limited to 'playthings' like motor cars, hi-fis and TV sets, but also include a greater quantity and quality of food. In general, this means more meat. This in turn means more production on the farm. This increased production can only be achieved by the application of more intensive methods of production, with more animals kept in a smaller space. Problems arise from this and disease risks increase.

Salmonella, the Food Poisoner
Report published by the British Association for the Advancement of Science
1975/1977

September 10

Generally, one joins a yoga society in order to improve his health, to reduce fat. People in rich nations eat more, become fat, and then pay exorbitant prices to so-called yoga instructors in order to reduce. People try to reduce by all these artificial gymnastics; they do not understand that if they just eat vegetables or fruits and grains, they will never get fat. People get fat because they eat voraciously, because they eat meat. People who eat voraciously suffer from diabetes, overweight, heart attacks etc, and those who eat insufficiently suffer from tuberculosis. Therefore moderation is required and moderation in eating means that he eat only what is needed to keep body and soul together.

A C BHAKTIVEDANTA. SWAMI PRABHUPADA
The Path to Perfection

September 11

Vegetarianism brings with it a new relationship to food, plants and nature. Flesh taints our meals. Disguise it as we may, the fact remains that the centrepiece of our dinner has come to us from the slaughter-house, dripping blood. Untreated and unrefrigerated, it soon begins to putrefy and stink. When we eat it, it sits heavily in our stomachs, blocking our digestive processes until, days later, we struggle to excrete it. When we eat plants, food takes on a different quality. We take from the earth food that is ready for us and does not fight against us as we take it. Without meat to deaden the palate there is an extra delight in fresh vegetables taken straight from the ground . . . I found the idea of picking my own dinner so satisfying that shortly after becoming a vegetarian I began digging up part of our backyard and growing some of my own vegetables . . . dropping flesh-meat from my diet brought me into closer contact with plants, the soil, and the seasons.

PETER SINGER 1946–
Australian writer and professor of philosophy involved with the Australian Animal Liberation Movement
Animal Liberation
Random House NY USA 1975 & Jonathan Cape UK 1990

September 12

Vegetarians always ask about getting enough protein. But I don't know any nutrition expert that can plan a diet of natural foods resulting in a protein deficiency, so long as you're not deficient in calories. You need only six per cent of total calories in protein . . . and it's practically impossible to get below nine per cent in ordinary diets.

NATHAN PRITKIN
American nutritionist

September 13

I always speak with the greatest delight and satisfaction in the presence of my friends the members of the Vegetarian Society. With them I have no dissatisfaction. This is not the case when I speak for my friends the Anti-Vivisectionists, the Anti-Vaccinationists, the Spiritualists, or the advocates of Freedom for Women. I always feel that such of these as are not abstainers from flesh-foods have unstable ground under their feet, and it is my great regret that, when helping them in their good works, I cannot openly and publicly maintain what I so ardently believe—that the vegetarian movement is the bottom and basis of all other movements towards Purity, Freedom, Justice and Happiness.

ANNA KINGSFORD MD 1846–1888
An Address to the Vegetarian Society

September 14

Just as we slander people we have wronged by attaching to them such labels as 'congenitally lazy', 'stupid', or 'dirty', or 'barbarous', to justify our oppression and/or exploitation of them, in the same way, we denigrate animals we want to slaughter in order to eat them with an untroubled conscience. And so the pig, which is a relatively clean animal, is labeled 'dirty swine', the cow 'bovine'—a term implying stupidity and unfeelingness—and the whale 'killer'. (Is there a more pervasive killer than civilized man?) On top of that we invent euphemisms like 'ham', 'pork', 'steak', 'beef', 'veal', 'mutton', so we won't be reminded that we are ingesting the scorched flesh of dead pigs, cows, calves, and sheep, slain for the pleasures of our palates. In fact the word 'meat' itself is a euphemism. Originally referring to solid food, as in the expression 'meat and drink' it later came to mean the flesh of an animal.

ROSHI PHILIP KAPLEAU 1912–
A Buddhist Case For Vegetarianism
Rider 1983

September 15

We, human beings, should establish the World Federation to keep a lasting world peace by the constitution. However, we should not be satisfied with only human peace. We should be conscious of human responsibility to all living things.

By way of science and education, not of law, we should make our utmost effort rapidly to stop the killing of higher animals by humans on the earth.

Furthermore, we should fulfil 'All Human's Responsibility to All Living Things', making efforts to stop the killing of the lower animals.

To realize this high purpose, the World Federation Government should do its best to study science and promote education.

HISATOKI KOMAKI PHD
Founder-President of the Hisatoki Komaki Foundation for the Peace of All Spiritual Beings; pacifist and Nobel prize candidate
Article 83: *Humankind's Responsibility to All Living Things* from Joint Proposition to the Draft of the World Federation Constitution, August 6th 1981

September 16

We shall have our reward, even on earth, for following St Francis and becoming aware of the goodness of God in all His creation. Like him (in the words of Pope Pius XI) we shall 'be led to love all things which we know have the same principle of life as ourselves and in which we recognize the goodness of God. We shall follow our Well-Beloved everywhere and in every trace of Him to be found in His creatures. And thus we shall learn to make of all things about us a ladder to reach His throne.'

Draft for Sermon at Westminster Cathedral to have been given by The Very Reverend Ambrose Agius OSB 2.10.1977

☙ ☜

September 17

The great-hearted G K Chesterton looked on all creatures with the eyes of their Creator and saw that they were good. In the course of a memorable essay on the much-slandered pig he wrote: 'I never could imagine why pigs should not be kept as pets. To begin with, pigs are very beautiful animals. Those who think otherwise are those who do not look at anything with their own eyes, but through other people's eyeglasses. The actual lines of a pig (I mean a really fat pig) are among the loveliest and most luxuriant in nature. If we could but rid ourselves of old prejudices, and look at things as they are and not as they are said to be, pigs on pedestals might come to rival the Venus de Milo, with the added advantage of being whole and entire!'

LIAM BROPHY 1910-
A Poke at the Pig
The Ark August 1984 (Journal of the Catholic Study Group for Animal Welfare)

September 18

The Four Stages of Cruelty were done in hopes of preventing in some degree that cruel treatment of poor animals which makes the streets of London more disagreeable to the human mind than anything whatever, the very describing of which gives pain.

WILLIAM HOGARTH   1697–1764
English painter and engraver; satirist.
On his engravings: *The Four Stages of Cruelty*

September 19

During Dr Johnson's visit to Gwaynynog, Wales, the gardener caught a hare in the potato plants. When Johnson heard it was to be taken to the cook, he asked to have it put into his arms, and then immediately dropped it out of the window, shouting after it to accelerate its speed. Reproached by his host, John Myddleton, for having lost what promised to be an excellent dinner, he replied, 'So much the better, Sir, for if your table is to be supplied at the expense of the laws of hospitality, I envy not the appetite of him who eats it. This, Sir, is not a *hare ferae naturae*, but one which has placed itself under your protection and savage indeed must be the man who does not make his hearth an asylum for the confiding stranger.'

DR SAMUEL JOHNSON   1709–1784
English essayist, lexicographer, poet and moralist
Dr Johnson & the Hare
The European Magazine 1798

September 20

. . . It is a depraving tendency, sadly common with English lads, to desire to kill a beautiful animal the moment they see it. That the first thought on discovering a new creature should be 'is it nice to eat?' is to one shocking and debasing. What is called the love of sport has become a love of killing for the display of skill, and converts man into the tyrant of all other animals; yet this rose out of a desire of eating their flesh—a desire which cannot be blamed in that state of barbarism in which little other food was to be had. But when with the growth of civilization other food is easier to get, when bread has won upon flesh-meat, it is evil to struggle for the more barbarous state. Does not the love of flesh inflame the love of killing, teach disregard for animal suffering, and prepare men for ferocity against men?

FRANCIS WILLIAM NEWMAN 1805–1897
English scholar and man of letters; brother of Cardinal Newman
Essays on Diet

September 21

We must attain the goal of the Total Disarmament of the World (World Federation) as soon as possible.

We must attain the goal of VEGETARIANISM as soon as possible, too.

. . . One of the most important purposes of the Total Disarmament of the World and that of VEGETARIANISM are all mankind's powerful PRAYER for the eternal happiness of all spiritual beings of the eternal and infinite Universe (Not only Earth).

. . . I believe that the Universal Life is not only the Universal Law (Will) but also the Universal PERSONA possessing the Infinite Love, Wisdom and Power. And therefore, all spiritual beings must be immortal and must evolve to be completely happy. If not, the infinite Universe is the infinite wickedness.

HISATOKI KOMAKI PHD
Why I am a Christian as Well as a Vegetarian
Lecture 1981

September 22

'Working with three guns and two loaders, he once had seven pheasants dead in the air at once; killed 28 birds in a minute, and 894 birds in a day.' Such was the life of the gentry in the 19th Century, and in parts of England it's not all that different today. Did not the newspapers record a few days ago that Prince Philip killed 5,000 pheasants in one recent year? The first gunman mentioned above was Earl de Gray, later, Second Marquess of Ripon, and the statistics set out were in *The Guardian* yesterday.

The information comes originally from fifty-three books—game books, some call them—which record his shooting exploits over a lifetime and which are to be sold at Sotheby's next month. His shooting career lasted from 1867 to 1923, and, *The Guardian* guesses, he slaughtered in all something like half a million creatures.

The Irish Times   15.2.1986

☙ ☞

September 23

THE PUZZLED GAME-BIRDS

They are not those that used to feed us
When we were young—they cannot be—
These shapes that now bereave and bleed us?
They are not those who used to feed us?
For would they not fair turns concede us?
If hearts can house such treachery
They are not those who used to feed us
When we were young—they cannot be!

THOMAS HARDY 1840–1928
English novelist and poet

September 24

You will observe that our Lord is called a Lamb . . . that title was as defenceless and as innocent as a lamb is . . . Now what is it that moves our very hearts and sickens us so much as cruelty shown to poor animals? I suppose this first, that they have done no harm; next that they have no power whatsoever of resistance; it is the cowardice and tyranny of which they are the victims which makes their sufferings so especially touching . . .

. . . there is something so very dreadful, so satanic in tormenting those who have never harmed us, and who cannot defend themselves, who are utterly in our power, who have weapons neither of offence nor defence, that none but very hardened persons can endure the thought of it.

CARDINAL NEWMAN 1801–1890
English churchman and writer; leader of the Oxford Movement
Extract from a sermon

September 25

While Moses was tending the sheep of Jethro in the Wilderness, a lamb was separated from the flock. He ran after it until it reached Ha Shuah where it came upon a pool of water and stopped to drink. When Moses reached it, he said, 'I did not know that you were thirsty and you must be tired.' He placed the lamb on his shoulder and began to walk. The Holy One, Blessed be He said, 'Because you have shown compassion to a little lamb you are fit to lead my children, Israel.'

Exodus. Rabbah 2:2
Reprinted in *Jewish Vegetarian,* March 1988

September 26

I do not like eating meat because I have seen lambs and pigs killed. I saw and felt their pain. They felt the approaching death. I left in order not to see their death. I could not bear it. I cried like a child. I ran up a hill and could not breathe. I felt that I was choking. I felt the death of the lamb.

VASLAV NIJINSKY 1890–1950
Russian ballet dancer and choreographer
Diary of Vaslav Nijinsky ed Romola Nijinsky
Cape 1937

September 27

Pensioners on a council estate for old people are rapidly turning vegetarian as they have become upset by the noise and smells from the Quantock foods abattoir situated only fifty yards from their homes in Little Britain, Dorchester.

One resident said, 'Six nights out of seven we are unable to sleep as the poor creatures for slaughter bellow incessantly all night.' Another resident said, 'It's worse for people in the first floor flats overlooking the yard. They can see what's going on as well as having to put up with the noise and smell.' Another resident said, 'It's really awful, so bad we are all becoming vegetarians.'

Their petitions to West Dorset Environmental and Public Health Committee have fallen on deaf ears. As the Dorset Evening Echo says, 'They will have to learn to live with it.'

JOYCE D' SILVA
General manager, Compassion in World Farming
Agscene 1988

September 28

The dissolution of commercial animal farming as we know it obviously requires more than our individual commitment to vegetarianism. To refuse on principle to buy products of the meat industry is to do what is right, but it is not to do enough. To recognize the rights of animals is to recognize the related duty to defend them against those who violate their rights, and to discharge this duty requires more than our individual abstention. It requires acting to bring about those changes that are necessary if the rights of these animals are not to be violated. Fundamentally, then, it requires a commitment to contribute to the revolution in our culture's thought about, and in its accepted treatment of, farm animals . . .

But prejudices die hard, all the more so when . . . they are insulated by widespread secular customs and religious beliefs, sustained by large and powerful economic interests, and protected by the common law. To overcome the collective entropy of these forces-against-change will not be easy. The animal rights movement is not for the faint heart.

TOM REGAN 1938-
American Professor of Philosophy
The Case for Animal Rights
Routledge Keagan Paul 1984

September 29

Most humans are locked in false inhibiting concepts: they believe that animal products are necessary for health. The opposite is true, animals yield nothing, not even fertilizer for the soil, that cannot be got more efficiently from plants. On the contrary, the second population of deliberately bred animals competes with the human for plant foods and vital diminishing resources of land, water, energy research skills . . . Their increasingly cruel exploitation threatens just retribution.

Vegans prompted by disinterested compassion have demonstrated the validity of the vegan way for individual human health. Can they now learn, and teach, that veganism is equally vital for the health of the planet. Can carnivorous humans be freed from the habits and thought patterns of millenia? Can vegans free themselves from the false values and practices of the consumer society and turn 'green'?

KATHLEEN JANNAWAY 1915–
The Vegan Winter 1990

September 30

Last year we ate 2,500,000 cows. 450,000,000 chickens, 25,000,000 turkeys, 14,000,000 sheep, 13,000,000 pigs, 8,000,000 ducks, 3,000,000 rabbits and 1,000,000 quail were slaughtered to feed us—and our pets.

ANNE BOSTON
Country Living May 1990

October 1

The memories of one Maryland chicken slaughterhouse will always be with me. It was summer, 90 degrees heat, humid, no shade, and the chickens were in stacked crates. As we walked in, we were breathing the palpable stench of warm, dying bodies. It soaked through our clothes and skin. We took some birds out of the crates, and they tried to drink melting ice from our hands. They were too weak to keep their heads up. They would have stayed there until the next morning, dying of heat prostration, respiratory failure and so on. We made the security guards call in the manager to finish them off. It's the closest I've ever been to Auschwitz.

INGRID NEWKIRK
American founder of People For the Ethical Treatment of Animals (PETA) USA
Interview reproduced in *In Defence of Animals*
Basil Blackwell 1985

October 2

Puir battery-hens
Ken nae sunlicht,
Nor see the stars . . .
Lang, lang the nicht.

JAMIE A SMITH 1910-
Scottish poet, vegetarian and anti-vivisectionist. Winner of the Scottish Open Poetry Competition 1986.
The Ark April 1978, Vol XLVI No 1
(Journal of the Catholic Study Group for Animal Welfare)

October 3

Fruit bears the closest relation to light. The sun pours a continuous flood of light into the fruits, and they furnish the best portion of food a human being requires for the sustenance of mind and body.

AMOS BRONSON ALCOTT 1799–1888
American philosopher, teacher and poet

October 4

As vegans, we have a uniquely important role—our diet is the only one which helps to reduce the greenhouse effect. All others add to it—carnivorism most of all! Everybody who reduces their animal flesh and dairy product intake helps to reduce global warming. Vegetarians, by consuming milk, cheese and possibly butter, besides supporting the cruellest and most unnatural life of a cow and calf, are just as big a burden on land usage as carnivores. We must get rid of cattle and sheep (for food) as fast as we possibly can, worldwide—and plant trees instead!

. . . The universal adoption of the vegan diet would release enough land for the massive re-afforestation needed to mop up CO_2. It is the only diet which could also remove 20-25% of all CH_4 (methane).

EDWARD SMAIL 1918-
Long-standing vegan
Veganism and the Greenhouse Effect
The Vegan, Summer 1990

October 5

In the USA the meat industry is the second largest manufacturing and processing concern (the largest is the manufacture of cars) and worth approximately $50 billion a year. It plays a prominent role in other countries' economics as well. Large scale fishing is of primary economic importance in much of the Third World, and significant in developed countries. Related industries, such as steel production and pharmaceutical manufacture, dramatically increase the meat and fish producers' influence and power. The steel industry supplies cages and machinery for ·factory farms, while *more then half the world's production of antibiotics is used in medicated animal feeds.*

But these statistics need not be disheartening. However great its size, the farm animal industry is extremely vulnerable to the threat posed to its continued existence by public compassion for the animals it victimizes.

HARRIET SCHLEIFER 1952–
In Defence of Animals (ed Peter Singer)
Basil Blackwell 1985

October 6

CHATTEL

Driving back from the literature festival
through Otley handsome in black stone
With white revers of painted windows and doors
I follow behind a tin truck
gaping an open vent high up at the back.
Stopped at the lights the gap is filled
with broad snout, a wet black sponge for sucking up
sweetness from deep in summer grass.
You crane your head in the hole sideways to let
each eye in turn roll up at the sky.
Deep in tumbril shock you don't speak.
I know where you're going this summer's morning
and feel you know it too though how
when no one has ever come back with telltale
smell of blood and fear on staring hide?
I image though I can't see the shrunken dug
flat as a perished rubber glove.
The street is called Wharfdale View. It looks across
to where the moors throw a green quilt
for miles under a high sky. Why can't I just
draw the steel bolt on the tailgate
and let you run and run up there till you drop?
But the lights change. You turn Left; I go Right
for Leeds and perhaps I'm quite wrong
and you're just being moved on to new pasture.
Then why can't I safe home sleep
but see still your face laid along the tailgate
with one moist eye turned up questioning
whether I would have drawn that bolt
if you'd been able to ask me in a tongue
I couldn't kid myself I misunderstood.

MAUREEN DUFFY 1933–
English poet, novelist, playwright and non-fiction writer
Collected Poems
Hamish Hamilton 1985

October 7

The Australian Free the Battery Hen Association has offered $A1,500 to any battery farmer who will swap places with one of his hens for a week. He will be called on to live for the week in a scaled up battery cage. Presumably feeding and toilet-use will be catered for in the cage, but NO bed on the grounds that the hens get neither nest nor perch.

Agscene No 98 Spring 1990

October 8

CON'S PLACE
(for Irmhilt de Matté)

They ate meat at that place,
Con, offspring, wife and cat;
Bins of skin and bones,
A baby slow and fat.

The sink was lined with grease.
To Holy Rome in thrall,
When he pounded steak
Blood spattered on the wall.

Whilst I was lodger there
An opportunist mouse
Nightly re-emerged
To snack about the house.

Blessed Crucifixes:–
One overhung my bed,
Twisting Jesu's wounds
Unexpurgated red.

Inclining heavenwards,
Pope John exerts control:
'Corpses for table
Lack our immortal soul.'

May such achieve aloft
Gold harps, angelic wings.
Please recycle me
With earth's four-footed things.

DENNIS JONES MD
1993

October 9

SEASONS
(for T and AV)

Yesterday they were separated. All night
lambs' long thin baas have woven with ewes'
deep piled lows a mat of grieving over late
summer fields slubbed with drought's succulent dews.

Martins hammer at the eaves still. The swifts
have sailed for Egypt and sickle swallows home
away. Trunks are packed; new gym shoes etch sharp prints.
Fresh cut ridges lie marled with sour pig dung

for the plough's knife. The sheep fall silent then let
a bitter reprise loose in the milk rinsed dawn
for the rubbery snuggle of lips and teat.
The ewes' bellies will swell with those to be born.
Autumn sounds a new sprung stave for them to learn
but the lambs' fate is tabled. Some things never return.

MAUREEN DUFFY 1933–
Collected Poems 1949–84
Hamish Hamilton

October 10

In our mind's eye the farm is a peaceful, pleasant place where calves muzzle their mothers in a shady field, pigs loaf in the mudhole and chickens scratch and scramble about the barnyard. We comfort ourselves with these bucolic images—images that are implanted by calendars, colouring books and the countrified labelling and advertising of animal products.

The reality of modern animal production, however, is starkly different from these scenes. Now, virtually all of our poultry products and about half of our milk and red meat come from animals mass-produced in huge factory-like systems. In some of the more intensively managed 'confinement' operations, animals are crowded in pens and cages stacked up like so many shipping crates. On these factory farms there are no pastures, no streams, no seasons, not even day and night. Health and productivity come not from frolics in sunny meadows but from syringes and additive-laced food.

JIM MASON 1950–
American attorney and free-lance journalist with especial interest in rural life
Brave New Farm? In Defence of Animals (ed Peter Singer)
Blackwell

October 11

G F Newman likes to shock. Politics? 'I'm a progressive vegan,' says the TV dramatist. So much so that he only allowed vegan food at the press review for his latest drama series *For the Greater Good*, and will not wear leather, hence his canvas shoes.

G F NEWMAN (interviewed by Richard Brooks)
British novelist, playwright, TV dramatist, screenwriter
The Observer March 1991

'I'm not foaming at the mouth with anger. Nor am I driven by class prejudice; nor do I take a left/right position. People say to me, "Well, what are you? . . ." I'm a radical vegan.'

'What stems from that is non-exploitation. The exploitation of animals paves the way for all others. We can't secure rights for women, gays, children, old people or anyone else in isolation. We have to have rights for everyone, and that includes animals.'

G F NEWMAN (interviewed by David James Smith)
Guardian March 1991

October 12

The assumption that animals are without rights and the illusion that our treatment of them has no moral significance is a positively outrageous example of Western crudity and barbarity. Universal compassion is the only guarantee of morality.

ARTHUR SCHOPENHAUER 1788–1860
German philosopher

October 13

Our friend, (Frey Ellis) was a consultant haematologist in a busy general hospital; his greatness lay rather in the warmth of his friendship, and his persistent determination, in spite of a heavy load of routine work, to follow a line of research which to many would have seemed unattractive and unlikely to yield useful results.

. . . Frey Ellis was himself a vegan and had been so for over twenty years. People adopt a vegetarian or vegan diet for various reasons—a love of animals, health, economy, cultural pressures and religious beliefs. Frey Ellis thought deeply and had a real interest in life and living things. But beyond all this he was a doctor, and his vision was to see in plant foods a possible answer to some of the ills to which we in this country are subject and also a potential for solving the food problems of developing countries.

J W T DICKERSON PHD FIBIOL
Professor of Human Nutrition, University of Surrey
Plant Foods and Human Health. The 1979 Frey Ellis Memorial Lecture
The Vegan Society 1979

October 14

The nobler a soul is, the more objects of compassion it hath.

FRANCIS BACON 1561–1626
English philosopher, essayist and statesman

October 15

The brute animals have all the same sensations of pain as human beings, and consequently endure as much pain when their body is hurt; but in their case the cruelty of torment is greater, because they have no mind to bear them up against their sufferings and no hope to look forward to when enduring the last extreme pain . . .

THOMAS CHALMERS 1780–1847
Scottish divine and writer, philosopher, reformer

October 16

Man has a natural tendency to seek power over others, hence, if they are weaker so much the better. As a consequence the cruelty inflicted is proportional to the status of the victim. Animals have no real status and so are treated with more cruelty more often.

It is and always has been their lot to be exploited . . . As it is undesirable for men to be cruel, these traits have to be curbed. This is necessary as in harming animals they ultimately harm themselves. Whether from self-interest or altruism, the usual method is by legislation . . . Granting animal rights will in turn strengthen human rights. Ultimately the fate of man and animal is inextricably linked. In the mystery of living their destinies are interdependent, interrelated and interwoven. Law as man's mirror of morality should reflect and respect that basic truth.

NOEL SWEENEY LLB
English barrister
Animals, Cruelty and the Law
Alibi 1990

October *17*

The reasons for legal intervention in favour of children apply not less strongly to the case of those unfortunate slaves and victims of the most brutal part of mankind—the lower animals.

JOHN STUART MILL 1806–1873
English philosopher and economist
The Principle of Political Economy 1848

October *18*

To say that you behaved like animals is offensive to the animal creation because animals of the farmyard and field have an innate sense of decency.

MR JUSTICE CUSSACK
at Leeds Assizes, UK 1971

October 19

We cannot doubt that if Man had always limited himself to the use of the nourishment destined by nature for his organs, he would not be seen today to have become the victim of this multitude of maladies which, by a premature death, makes a harvest of the greater number of individuals before age or Nature has put bounds to the career of his life . . .

Men . . . coming from the hands of Nature, lived a long time without thinking of immolating living things to gratify their appetite. They are, without doubt, those happy times which our ancient poets have represented to us under the agreeable allegory of the *Golden Age*. In fact, Man, by natural organization, mild, nourishing himself only on vegetable foods, must have been originally of pacific disposition, quite fitted to maintain among his fellows that happy peace which makes the delight of Society . . .

JEAN BAPTISTE PRESSAVIN 1760–1830
L'art de Prolonger la Vie et de Conserver la Santé

October 20

Even when furnishings remained simple it is probable that the middle-classes, as well as their betters, over-ate. Men like Parson Woodforde, whose diary in this, as in so many aspects of 18th Century life, illuminates the domestic practices of his age, dilates, with obvious satisfaction, on the pleasures of the table, recording with loving care his consumption of roast duck, of roasted swan, of a pike 'with a Pudding in his Belly' . . . serving gooseberries with roast pork . . .

DOROTHY MARSHALL
English People in the 18th Century
1956

October 21

THE BUNCH OF LARKS

Portly he was, in carriage somewhat grand;
  Of gentleman he wore the accepted marks:
He trod the busy street, and in his hand
  He bore a bunch of larks!

I met him in the street, and turn'd about,
  And mused long after he had flaunted by.
A bunch of larks! and his intent, no doubt,
  To have them in a pie.

Yes, four and twenty larks baked in a pie!
  O, what a feast of melody is there!
The ringing chorus of a summer sky!
  A dish of warbling air!

How many dusty wanderers of the earth
  Have still'd voices lifted from the dust!
And now to end their almost heavenly mirth
  Beneath a gourmand's crust!

But as he picks their thin ambrosial throats,
  Will no accusing memories arise,
Of grassy glebes, and heaven-descending notes,
  And soul-engulfing skies?

'Give me,' cries he, 'the *substance* of a thing—
  Something that I can eat, or drink, or feel—
A poem for the money it will bring—
  Larks for the dainty meal.'

Well, he may have his substance, and I mine.
  Deep in my soul the throbbing lark-notes lie.
My substance lasts, and takes a life divine—
  His passes with the pie.

ROBERT LEIGHTON 1611–1684
Archbishop of Glasgow, author and peacemaker
Accounted a saint from youth

October 22

Birds and beasts have no divine incarnation to guide them, for they have no inclination to stray away from their *dharma* (right living, self-disciplinary rules). Man alone forgets or ignores the goal of life.

SAI BABA 1926–
Sai Baba, The Embodiment of Love
Sawbridge Enterprises 1982

October 23

To those who, while considering themselves spiritually-minded, some-times put forward the fallacious viewpoint that animals were placed on earth for man's use (meaning abuse, and to eat), Baba states quite categorically: 'Animals did not come for the purpose of supplying food for human beings. They came to work out their own lives in the world. When a human being is dead the foxes and other animals may eat the dead body; we have not come for that purpose. Similarly, man eats the animal, but the animal has not come to provide man with food. But we have taken to eating meat as a habit'. (When Baba says 'we' he refers, of course, to human beings in general, for even as a small child he would not remain in a house where flesh was cooked.)

PEGGY MASON and RON LAING MA
Sai Baba devotees
Sai Baba, The Embodiment of Love
Gateway Books (4th Edition)

October 24

. . . It is estimated that in one year alone Britain imported groundnut protein from India to the equivalent of a year's ration for 13,000,000 children—and all to feed tormented factory-farm animals, which never so much as see the daylight until they are carted off, in fear, to be slaughtered.

By feeding this valuable food to a vast animal population a loss in protein value in excess of 80% is incurred in the end product. This same food, either in its original form or by simple processing for direct human consumption entails a loss of only 10–15%. Without this mania for consuming the corpses of countless millions of our gentle, vegetarian 'younger brothers' there would be enough food for all of us—and a great deal of disease would be eliminated.

PEGGY MASON and RON LAING MA
Sai Baba, The Embodiment of Love
Gateway Books (4th Edition)

∽ ∾

October 25

Many of our *Buddhist Perception of Nature* project's Tibetan research colleagues can point to the time, in living memory, when herds of wild blue sheep, yak, deer and flocks of migrating birds would travel with Tibetan nomads, or land in the midst of human settlements—apparently sensing they were safe. For the most part they were safe from harm, because the country was Buddhist.

The situation since the Chinese takeover has tragically changed . . .

DR CHATSUMARN KABILSINGH
Tree of Life. Buddhism and Protection of Nature
Buddhist Perception of Nature 1987

October 26

. . . Neither can anyone pretend that, in a confrontation between humans and the calves they propose to convert into roast veal, there is any question of Them or Us. The conspicuous and healthy existence of human vegetarians makes it impossible to claim that taking the calf's life is necessary to sustaining human life. And neither can the most practised voluptuary pretend that the fraction of his total pleasure in life that comes from eating the veal is larger than the fraction of the calf's total pleasure that would have come from its being allowed to continue its life . . . the moral position of the humans is straightforward. We simply override the others. Arbitrarily and wantonly—without, that is to say, justification or necessity—we are tyrants.

BRIGID BROPHY 1929
British writer, novelist and philosopher
In Pursuit of a Fantasy
Animals Men and Morals (ed Stanley & Roslind Godlovitch and John Harris)
Grove Press Inc NY, USA 1971

October 27

The cow (in a large herd in our industrialized agricultural system) will not find security in an established place in the herd hierarchy. Her agitation will be increased by the absence of any real relationship with the herdsman. She is pressed relentlessly for higher yields of milk. The energy dense rations that support those higher yields produce acid indigestion, and commonly, a range of clinical conditions from milk fever to mastitis. Hours spent on concrete floors may cripple the cow, her high energy diet will have predisposed her to lameness. Many dairy farmers rely on antibiotics to hold back the flood of diseases.

The New Scientist 29.9.1983

October 28

Those who supply our food use pure water at the incredible rate of a billion gallons every three minutes. That amounts to at least twenty times the volume of water used by households and it underlies the problem of a highly overtaxed national water supply. Compounding the problem are food producers themselves. Within their ranks are many ranchers and cattlemen who have resorted to overgrazing. Overgrazing is not only destroying vast expanses of our once-resplendent grasslands but it is causing water tables to plummet and thereby depleting the nation's water reserves.

Ironically, food producers pollute more water than they consume; they are directly responsible for more than half of all the nation's water pollution . . . feedlot operators and others who fatten livestock are responsible for more of the nation's water pollution than all of industry and all households combined. As if this were not enough, meat packers are the nation's principal industrial polluter.

ROBIN HUR
Vegetarianism For A World Of Plenty
Moneysworth March 1979
Reprinted and Distributed by Vegetarian Information Service. Box 5888, Washington DC

October 29

. . . We arrived. Even before entering we could smell the oppressive, detestable, rotten odor of joiner's glue or of glue paint . . . It is a very large red brick building with vaults and high chimneys. We entered through the gate . . . By the wall of the little house, and to the right of it, sat six butchers in aprons, which were covered with blood, with bloodspattered sleeves rolled up over muscular arms. They had finished their work about half an hour ago, so that on that day we could see only empty chambers. In spite of the gates being opened on two sides, there was in each chamber an oppressive odour of warm blood; the floor was cinnamon-coloured and shining, and in the depressions of the floor stood coagulated black gore.

One of the butchers told us how they slaughtered, and showed us the place where this is done. I did not quite understand him, and formed a false, but very terrible conception of how they slaughtered, and I thought, as is often the case, that the reality would produce a lesser effect upon me than what I had imagined. But I was mistaken in this . . .

LEO TOLSTOY 1828–1910
A visit to a slaughterhouse in Tiela
Preface to *The Ethics of Diet* 1892

October 30

All beings hold themselves dear. Just as we want to live, so do our fellow creatures. How can we feel peaceful and happy about taking another's life, in order to sustain our own? Even a dog or a tiger has Buddha nature. Rabbits, birds, turtles—all are potential Buddhas. How can we kill and eat potential and future Buddhas? Living on the flesh of others cuts our seed of compassion. Do we really want to cause fear, pain, suffering and death, in order to satisfy a taste desire that vanishes as soon as it goes beyond our tongues?

As we—and all creatures—may have been each others' mothers, fathers, brothers, sisters, husbands, wives, sons and daughters, for countless lifetimes, how can we feast upon our past relatives? As we must maintain the body in order to realize our 'pure mind', vegetables, fruit and grains can supply our needs, and even for these we can feel deep gratitude. Give your seed of compassion a chance to sprout and grow by living in as harmless a manner as possible. You will begin to experience something wonderful—a oneness with all life!

BIK KHUNI MIAO KWANG SUDHARMA 1928–
The Source

~ ~

October 31

Pythagoras enjoined abstinence from the flesh of animals because this was conducive to Peace. Those who are accustomed to abominate the slaughter of other animals, as iniquitous and unnatural, will think it still more unlawful and unjust to kill a man or to engage in war. Especially he exhorted the politicians and legislators to abstain, for if they were willing to act justly, in the highest degree, it was indubitably incumbent upon them to not injure any of the lower animals, since how could they persuade others to act justly, if they themselves proved to be indulging an insatiable avidity by devouring those animals allied to us, since through the communion of life and the same elements, and the sympathy existing, they are as it were conjoined to us by a fraternal alliance.

IAMBLICHUS c. 250–325
Neoplatonist philosopher
De Vita Pythagorica

November 1

Hast thou named all the birds without a gun?
Loved the wood-rose, and left it on its stalk?
At rich man's tables eaten bread and pulse?
Unarmed, faced danger with a heart of trust?
Oh, be my friend, and teach me to be thine.

RALPH WALDO EMERSON 1803–1882

November 2

... But this was the greatest pollution among men, to devour the goodly
limbs (of animals) whose life they had reft from them.

EMPEDOCLES OF AGRIGENTUM fl. 444 or 460 BC
Greek philosopher interested in biology, medicine and physics
From the poem *Katharmoi (Purifications)*

November 3

Else they are all—the meanest things that are,
As free to live, and to enjoy that life,
As God was free to form them at the first
Who in His sovereign wisdom made them all.
Ye therefore who love mercy, teach your sons to love it too.

WILLIAM COWPER 1731–1800
English pre-Romantic poet and hymn writer

November 4

At a sale in August a mare with her foal (which was estimated to be about three months old) entered the ring. Only the foal was offered for sale and she was bought for meat at 55 guineas. At Brigg Fair a mare, six years old, and her filly foal by a thoroughbred stallion went for slaughter at 230 guineas. (The two were rescued by a horse rescue society.) There is no doubt that the majority of unbroken ponies which are auctioned in Wales, the New Forest and Dartmoor, will go for meat.

PETER HUNT
Hon. Sec. Bransby Home of Rest for Horses
Address to Board Meeting of Animal Welfare Year (August 17th 1977)

November 5

A man who is kind to the animals belonging to him will be thoughtful of the feelings and wishes of his family. A woman who, with patience and tenderness, cares for the domestic creatures around her home, can but be loving to her little ones; for she must observe how strong is the mother-love in the humblest thing that lives.

MRS F A F WOOD-WHITE
Quoted in *Inmates of My House and Garden* by Eliza Brighton (naturalist)
T Fisher Unwin London 1895

~·~

November 6

. . . After a long series of events we were, much to our surprise, shown into one of these animal Belsens.

The house was large and, as we entered, we saw stretching before us a long avenue on both sides of which were several tiers of cages imprisoning thousands of hens. Clare and I both felt that we could not go beyond a few yards. The stench was almost unbearable and we felt that we could not get our breath. Flies were so numerous that we had to bat them away from our faces. There was a 'lagoon' (shame on the industry for using this lovely word in such a context) underneath the cages. These dung heaps are cleaned out only once a year. The birds were crammed in so that they could not move. My most vivid memory of the visit is of a hen who was in the end cage constantly moving her foot in a vain endeavour to find a spot on which to put it down. She could not. I cannot forget her.

VIOLET SPALDING
August 1977

November 7

In the early twelfth century the Cistercians were allowed two dishes of vegetables cooked without grease, and never took flesh meat of any kind . . . in 1237 the papal legate congratulated the English abbots on having passed a rule for entire abstinence from flesh meat . . . in the Carthusian houses in England flesh meat was not allowed, even to the sick and guests . . . and among the Grandmontines the flesh of birds, as well as quadrupeds, was definitely forbidden.

DEAN CRANAGE
The Home of the Monk

❧ ❨

November 8

. . . Even the Gospels themselves are full of Pauline influences. It is therefore in no way surprising to find that they are Pauline–to a limited extent– over the matter of meats. It is true that the Gospels never go so far as to say that the Master ate meat, but we have in Mark an astonishing passage (vii 14-15) . . . the reference to the Master's saying which is supposed to have sanctioned flesh-eating did not find its way into Mark's Gospel on the authority of Peter (who knew very well that the Master could have made no such absurd statement), but is an instance of the influence of the Pauline faction.

Thus an attempt of the Paulinists to pretend that the Master approved of flesh-eating has over-reached itself, and has revealed the glaring inconsistency of the records which purport to be reliable accounts of the Master's ministry and of the early days of Christianity.

REV HOLMES-GORE MA
Christ or Paul?
Renaissant Press, 10 De Vere Gardens London W8 5AE

November 9

The dolphin carries a loving affection not only unto man, but also to music; delighted is he with harmony in song, but especially with the sound of the water instrument, or such kind of pipes. Of man he is nothing afraid, neither avoideth him as a stranger; but of himself meeteth their ships, plaieth and disporteth himself and fetcheth a thousand frisks and gambols before them.

PLINY THE YOUNGER   AD 61–63
[Caius Plinius Caecilius Secundus]
Nephew and adopted son of Pliny the Elder; Roman writer

November 10

Hunting of dolphins is abomination. A man
Who wilfully brings about their death,
Can approach the gods no more. They will
Not love him for his offerings. His touch
Pollutes their altars, and he defiles all
Those who live below his roof. As much
Do the gods loathe to have death's doom
Brought on these chieftains of the deep.

OPPIAN
Greek poet c. 200 AD

November II

Twenty minutes pass.

The whale's ribs become too heavy to move.
The whale's rib muscles give up their strength.
The air-valves collapse, admitting a rush of sea-water;
The whale's lungs flood.
She suffocates and dies,
Revolving slowly in the water
Leaving her white stomach exposed . . .

She is left to drift,
Rimmed with oil-slick and blood.

With no enemies in the sea
The whale is loth to believe in the attack,
As were the Indians, as were the Aborigines . . .

The whale is stuffed through manholes,
To be carved into a sodden mess by whirring knives . . .

For fish-bait;
For cattle-meal;
For the food supplies to fur-farms;
For dog-food;
For cat-food; . . .
For low-calorie cooking fat;
For shortening for bread, and pastry, and cakes; . . .
For steaks: sashiini slices and marinated yamotami, . . .
For whale-meat rissoles;
For whale-meat stew . . .

The sullen killing continues.
The killing of the largest creatures in the world.
It is unthinkingly supposed
That the rest of life will not be shrivelled in the process.

HEATHCOTE WILLIAMS
British writer and actor
Whale Nation
Jonathan Cape (1989)

November 12

All the great whales have been approachable and peaceable on their first encounter at sea with man; it is only from the agonizing experience of being hunted, and wounded with harpoon, lance or bullet that they become wary and flee at the appearance of motor boats and the sound of engines. As many filming skindivers have lately shown, you can swim close to almost any of the great cetaceans, even the notorious killer whale, and touch (occasionally ride upon the back of) an individual, provided you move gently and silently. The cetacean will look you in the eye if the water is clear; in any case even in murky water it will know much about you by measuring you accurately with its sonar scanner, which—it is now believed—informs it of your size, shape, density, heart-beat rate and attitude to other living creatures.

Having decided you are harmless, some cetaceans, especially the young and playful adolescents, will show curiosity . . . With very little encouragement some species will enjoy a game with you under water. Pliny and Aristotle were right— these lively sea-mammals carry a loving affection unto man.

RONALD M LOCKLEY
Naturalist and writer pioneer in wildlife studies
Whales, Dolphins and Porpoises
David & Charles 1979

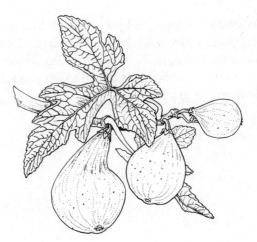

November 13

Many stories are told about the dolphin, indicative of his kind and gentle nature, and manifestations of passionate attachment to boys, in and about Taras, Karia and other places. One story goes that, after a dolphin had been caught and wounded off the coast of Karia, a school of dolphins came into the harbour and stopped there until the fisherman let his captive free;whereupon the school departed.

On one occasion a school of dolphins, large and small, was seen, and two dolphins appeared swimming underneath a little dead dolphin each time it was sinking, and supported it on their backs, trying out of compassion to prevent its being devoured by some predacious fish.

PLINY THE ELDER   AD 23–79
[Gaius Plinius Secundus]
Latin writer and natural sciences researcher

☙ ☞

November 14

A mother dusky (dolphin) whose calf had died in a fishing net in Hawke's Bay would not leave her child, which drifted ashore. She remained close by, though she could hear no sound from the dead calf, and eventually, . . . she lost the will to live, and died–there is no other explanation– of grief.

RONALD M LOCKLEY
Whales, Dolphins & Porpoises
David & Charles 1979

November 15

The usual method of capture in the harbour was to hook a dolphin with a gaff, tie a rope round its tail, hoist it on deck and slit its throat. Alternatively, many dolphins were hauled into the boat simultaneously in a net. Often the gaffed dolphins escaped to suffer from their wounds until finally caught. The killed dolphins were brought to the processing plant to be gutted and frozen or filleted. Around the plant were mounds of heads and tails connected by a meatless spine and interspersed with intestines. The harbour was red with blood from the slaughtered dolphins and from the crimson liquid continually flowing from the drain pipes of the processing plant. If too many dolphins were caught to be processed in one day, the survivors were left for the next . . .

Futo had a few hundred dolphins in the harbour, barricaded by nets . . . I learned it was to be the last hunt of the season . . . I saw what had to be done . . . The net was tied along the cement breakwater for a distance of about 50 feet . . . I proceeded to crawl along untying the net . . . The dolphins began jumping in the air . . . It was beautiful to watch . . . I watched half a dozen dolphins swim through the opening and dived into the water and swam into the harbour trying to communicate . . . the way to freedom was clear.

Swimming in the cold dark water with dolphins all around me and knowing I had accomplished what I set out to do was something I thank the Creator for letting me experience.

PATRICK WALL
Dolphin Rescue at Izu (Japan)
The Beast Summer 1981

November 16

The *Sea Shepherd* is avenged! Make no mistake about it—this was no accident, this was a deliberate act of sabotage! The Sierra will kill no more whales! . . . And there was more . . . All of these actions, I am proud to say , took place without loss of life or injury to the crews of the ships involved.

Yet, cetaceans continue to be killed along with other wild-life that are forced by man to die needlessly. Some six million dolphins have died in the last decade and a half after being netted by US tuna fishermen in the Eastern Pacific. Although the carnage has been reduced, over ten thousand are still being killed each year.

I have no death wish . . . I have fought with all my might to stay alive on those occasions that I felt death was near . . . But I must die some day. And when I do, an epitaph that said I fought to save the whales and the seals and all the creatures of the earth would not be too bad a thing.

That is what I will be doing—fighting for the whales until there are either no more whalers or no more whales. . . . We know what killing the whales is doing to the whales. But what is it doing to us?

PAUL WATSON
Canadian conservationist, rescuer of sea creatures with his boat, *Sea Shepherd*
Sea Shepherd: My Fight for Whales and Seals
W W Norton & Co NY & London 1979

November 17

The dolphin descends,
Swimming around you, mercurially,
And you pursue it again below.
It whirls and coils,
Describing three-dimensional hieroglyphs in its watery space
Then glances across at you.
A pencil thin stream of bubbles pours from its blow-hole
As it speaks.
Again, you are lost for a reply,
Immersed in this its element,
Knowing less than nothing.

Above the entrance
Of the oracle of its namesake, Delphi,
Was written the salutary phrase *Gnothee seauton*—Know thyself.
And all you know
Is that its serene assurance
Suggests that it knows exactly how to be a dolphin,
And few humans have the foresight to be human.

HEATHCOTE WILLIAMS
Falling for a Dolphin
Jonathan Cape 1988

November 18

HAIKU FOR A SPERM WHALE

Seed within a womb
of a womb that is the sea.
A whale is God's heart

LEN GASPIRINI
Whale Sound (Ed. Greg Gatenby)
J J Douglas Ltd Canada 1976

November 19

And lo, from the glinting rollers, haughtily rose the dolphin caparisoned with garish wreaths: it moved towards the girl who upright in the water, stripped of all her jewels, shone forth in the full lustre of her coal-black beauty and together they swam in the unearthly glare that foamed around their bodies. All of a sudden Shambowa grabbed the brute's back-fin and, with a wild cry, sprang astride on its hump. Against the gorgeous phosphorescence of the sea Camara saw Shambowa ride the huge fish exactly as in Italy in the museum near his birthplace he had seen Taras, the mythical founder of the town, bestride a leaping dolphin on the coins minted by the first Greeks who twenty-five centuries ago had settled on the shores of Tarentum's gulf.

Three days later when he awoke . . . Shambowa was shaking with fear and stretched unconscious at his side . . . After sunset . . . Shambowa . . . had romped with the dolphin . . . And now Shambowa was dying . . . They dug a grave on the cliff overhanging the beach . . .

Camara woke in the twilight of the dawn . . . He bolted out of the shed and the sight he saw was so ghastly that it chilled his spine . . .

Half-way between the shack and the sea, the dolphin was crawling, struggling with all its might on its flippers, dragging itself towards the shed in a pool of blood . . . Stormy petrels and seagulls were contending savagely for the daintiest bits . . .

He was sure that the dolphin had crawled on the beach trying to look for Shambowa: and dying in the hopeless enterprise, in a way it had found her.

ALBERTO DENTI DI PIRAJNO
Italian doctor who worked in Africa and later wrote of his experiences
A Grave for a Dolphin (Being an account of his Experiences in Africa)
Andre Deutsch 1956

November 20

I had spent the morning at a South of England abattoir watching truckloads of pigs being briskly slaughtered and was returning home when the bus was halted by a funeral procession . . . I could see the hearse with its polished coffin and gleaming brass rails, the half-dozen other hired limousines and, beyond them, a string of family saloons.

I'd seen 300 pigs go down that morning, creatures known in vivisection circles as 'horizontal man' because of the way the arrangement of their internal organs exactly matches our own; heart for heart, liver for liver, and because of that same warm, soft, slappy feeling to their bellies. I looked down at the creeping ceremonial marking the passage of one human and reflected on the neurotic haste with which the pigs had been killed: two and a half hours on the journey, then 15 minutes per animal, as it was electrocuted, stabbed, degutted and dispatched to the chillers . . . where the animals would not co-operate in their own slaughter—and even when they did—they were pushed, kicked, and cursed the way women are cursed: 'Come on, ya dozy bitch . . .'

What do you make of pigs? I had asked the slaughterman Barry Frame, some weeks earlier.

'Absolutely bloody stupid.'

'Why is that?'

'They've got a mind of their own. If they make up their mind they don't want to go where you want them to go, they won't.'

Britain kills fifteen million pigs a year.

ANDREW TYLER
British journalist
The Independent March 30th 1989

November 21

How To Calm Your Nerves

1. That which promotes human happiness is spiritual peace.
2. But happiness cannot easily be obtained if you do not discard obstinate bad habits, exchanging them for others which are truly good.
3. Abandon the inveterate habit of feeding on meat and fish.
4. Do not drink coffee and tea.
5. Do not drink alcohol: wine, beer, liqueurs. Don't feed yourself erroneously, on ham, salami or cheese sandwiches.
6. Don't suppress your blood pressure with daily drugs.
7. Begin your improvement by honestly dwelling upon world peace.
8. Quieten all the negative and hybrid passions in your heart.
9. Love that which is beautiful and raise a smile when you can, like the sun.
10. Fruit, flowers, orchards, gardens, mountains, valleys and rivers are beautiful.
11. The basest depths of human society are slaughterhouses: butchers' shops and meat markets, miserable dens of putrefaction, detestable and abominable.
12. Be on guard against all meals in which corpses have been cooked: pieces of meat, bits of intestine, brains of poor animals sacrificed, for the 'delight of the palate'.
13. Take celery salads and calm your nerves.
14. Drink, each morning, on rising, pure lemon juice.
15. Sleep, each night, in a contented world without violent tensions.
16. Your heart's peace and easy conscience are the timepiece of LIFE; adjust it to the right time now.

PROFESSOR N CAPO
Regenerate! Curate! (translated by Rebecca Hall)
Barcelona August 1975

November 22

During our Lamaze childbirth class there was a woman who came with her husband. The hunting season was due to start just when she was due to give birth. A few weeks before that the first deer (we named her Good Wild) came to the bottom of our garden, and lay there munching grass and flowers near the goldfish pond. I wrote a rare prose piece titled *Good Wild* with the nightmare ending of the hunter father shooting Good Wild as his wife gave birth to their baby.

FOUR DEER

They came softly in the grey dawn,
replacing the liquid melody of a solitary bird,
Four deer, fur the length and moistness
of the grass in the yard.

I left the curtain undrawn,
and caught the kettle before it whistled.

This morning I especially love
their long necks and the susceptible V of their ears,
their peace, their pride,
and above all, that they survive.

RICHARD MCKANE 1947–
British poet, Russian and Turkish translator and interpreter

November 23

. . . Male (red deer) calves are being factory farmed, the hinds are kept for the breeding herd. The male calves, after early weaning, are put into pens with small concrete yards attached, and are fed on a high concentrate ration together with straw and silage . . . each stag has about 21 square feet of living space in the pens . . .

There were 22,447 farmed deer in England and Wales in September (1988) . . . About 11,000 acres in the country have been fenced for deer farming. *The Scottish Farmer* reports that there are 17,000 farmed deer north of the border where there are nine herds of more than 200 hinds . . .

. . . Common market regulations . . . if introduced, would require all venison, whether farmed or shot in the wild, to be subject to the same meat inspection as other meats . . . if this European legislation goes through, it will probably mean abattoir slaughter in the long run for all deer . . .

Lord Massereene and Ferrand said that deer 'should never be sent to slaughterhouses because of their nervous disposition and acute sense of smell.' He added that they can certainly not be compared with cattle or pigs, which have been domesticated for thousands of years.

. . . The deer is a wild and timid species, and there are people about who want to subject it to growth-stimulative drugs, selective breeding, auction marts, long distance transport and expedient mutilations.

PETER ROBERTS
Agscene May/June and August/September 1989

November 24

The birds! The birds! How much happier would not my life on the beautiful island have been had I not loved them as I do! . . . For I know that the fair island that was a paradise to me was hell to them . . . They came just before sunrise. All they asked for was to rest for a while after their long flights across the Mediterranean . . . They came in thousands: woodpigeons, thrushes, turtle-doves, waders, quails, golden orioles, skylarks, nightingales, wagtails, chaffinches, swallows, warblers, redbreasts, and many other tiny artists on their way to give spring concerts to the silent forests and fields in the North. A couple of hours later they fluttered helplessly in the nets the cunning of man had stretched all over the island from the cliffs by the sea high up to the slopes of Monte Solaro and Monte Barbarossa. In the evening they were packed by hundreds in small wooden boxes without food and water and despatched by steamers to Marseilles to be eaten with delight in the smart restaurants of Paris. It was a lucrative trade, Capri was for centuries the seat of a bishop entirely financed by the sale of the netted birds.

AXEL MUNTHE 1857–1949
Swedish physician and writer
The Story of San Michele
John Murray Ltd

November 25

St. Guthlac . . . was in league with the fowls of the air; the wild birds . . . would eat from his hand; swallows came to sit on his arms and his bosom, and he said; 'He who is joined to God with a pure spirit finds all things uniting themselves to him in God.'

ROBERT G FOOKES

Extract from a letter to the Spectator July 19th 1890

St. Guthlac: born c. 673 died in 714. A hermit who cultivated close relationships with the birds and beasts and not complaining of the thieving habits of magpies and crows said, 'For men ought to set an example of patience even to wild creatures.'

November 26

The duck is considered a particularly uninteresting and prosaic animal. Yet I venture to affirm that, in point of intelligence, social kindness, and sagacity, he is vastly superior . . . I have witnessed striking instances of charity and kindness in ducks . . amongst some fifty or sixty . . . ducks and fowls, I once had a solitary little old bantam hen. She became blind, or nearly so, and like other birds in that condition . . . kept by herself in a dark retired corner of the fowl-house . . . Here she might, perhaps, have starved, but for the constant and sympathetic attentions of a duck. Twice daily, every day so long as the poor bantam lived, some three weeks, this good Samaritan . . . was observed to fill her capacious beak with from twenty to thirty grains of barley, with which she proceeded to the fowl-house, and there deposited her store immediately in front of the bantam. Several members of my family, as well as myself, were frequent witnesses to this beautiful incident.

SIDNEY M HAWKES
The Spectator May 10th 1884

November 27

Paté de foie gras is an expensive delicacy made from the swollen livers of geese which have been strapped into specially designed machines and force-fed three to four pounds of cooked maize a day. A commonly-voiced comment . . . is that this is equivalent to a human having to eat more than 28 pounds of spaghetti a day. At the end of the 25-day 'cramming' or 'gavage' period, the goose is killed and the liver removed. Often the liver is several times its natural size.

Before the bird is killed, however, its body has grown so distended that it can only breathe with great difficulty. According to the RSPCA, experiments on other ways of forcing geese to eat more food to enlarge the size of their livers have been carried out. They include surgery on the thyroid gland, which upsets the bird's 'satiety threshold' and also, it is understood, chemo-therapy.

CRAIG ANDERSON
Goose Cramming
The Beast Summer 1981

🐦 🐦

November 28

That it is easily possible to sustain life on the products of the vegetable kingdom needs no demonstration for physiologists, even if the majority of the human race were not constantly engaged in demonstrating it, and my researches show not only that it is possible, but that it is infinitely preferable in every way.

ALEXANDER HAIG MD FRS
Eminent physician and medical writer

November 29

It must be honestly admitted that, weight for weight, vegetable substances, when they are carefully selected, possess the most striking advantages over animal food in nutritive value . . . I should like to see the vegetarian and fruit-living plan brought into general use, and I believe it will be.

SIR BENJAMIN W RICHARDSON MD FRS   1828–1896
Physician, writer and sanitary reformer

November 30

American men killed in the Korean war showed, even at the age of twenty-two, striking signs of arteriosclerotic disease in their hearts as compared with Korean soldiers who were free of this damage to their blood vessels. The Americans were well fed with plenty of milk, butter, eggs and meat. The Koreans were basically vegetarians.

WILLIAM S COLLENS MD
Medical Counterpoint USA December 1989

December 1

It [flesh food] is material which of malice aforethought has sedulously been rendered toxic during the animal's lifetime. In the first place his endocrine defences are interfered with by castration; he is then immobilized and over-fed with a view to causing him to develop fatty degeneration of all his organs; and it is when this ugly process is complete that he is regarded as fit for human consumption.

DR LEONARD WILLIAMS
The Practitioner

December 2

Man by nature was never made to be a carnivorous animal, nor is he armed for prey or rapine, with jagged and pointed teeth, and claws to rend and tear; but with gentle hands to gather fruit and vegetables, and with teeth to chew and eat them.

JOHN RAY FRS

December 3

TO A FISH OF THE BROOK

Why fliest thou away with fear?
Trust me there's nought of danger near,
I have no wicked hook
All covered with a snaring bait,
Alas to tempt thee to thy fate,
And drag thee from the brook.

O harmless tenant of the flood,
I do not wish to spill thy blood,
For nature unto thee
Perchance hath given a tender wife,
And children dear, to charm thy life,
As she hath done to me.

Enjoy thy stream, O harmless fish;
And when an angler for his dish,
Through gluttony's vile sin,
Attempts, a wretch, to pull thee out,
God give thee strength, O gentle trout,
To pull the rascal in!

JOHN WOLCOT (PETER PINDAR) 1738–1819
English poet and physician

December 4

WHITEBAIT

Trawled out of the water's depth,
Deep, secret-dumb and out of reach
Where I hide my head in the ocean swell
Out of sight of daylight—the sun glare
Of the poised netting, the massed flickering
Silver squirming: drawn, dragged up out of sleep
Into the gulping and gull-circling air—
Thirty-five fish the length of a man
His hands slippery with scales, his eyes
Beaming deathlight on the catch
Slumping on the wet deck as they fall from me,
Their skinload leaving me standing

And then sitting, out of the dream here
As a plateful of them arrives in front of you:
Flour-coated, fried in seconds, dipped into the sun
Dunked, tipped and spread out with a fork
Among a few scraps of lettuce and lemon
To be speared one by one, crunched and consumed
By the mouth hardly even aware of them
As their fish-soul gathers and clouds my eyes
As I ask you how do you eat them? and you say
Heads, tails and all, go on, try one—
Fingering its tiny carcass by my thumb

Nipping it in half between my teeth
As the sea-swell rises behind my eyes
And I struggle to make this a matter of reverence
If I could swallow it whole I would, not
Wanting to break its gleaming wholeness
Brilliant, and quick-shoal darting, dead, here
In front of our unseeing eyes, hearts
Strangled like steaks in our stomachs . . .

JAY RAMSAY
British poet
From *Heart of Earth* (Book 6 of *The Great Return*)

December 5

The predatory life . . . brings little progress in social organization . . . Predaceous man unlike other forms of predatory life preys on his own species. With predaceous man civilization itself becomes of predatory type . . . Economic warfare, commercial warfare, class warfare, are symptomatic of *homo praedatorius*. He exploits cruelty on sub-human lives as well as on human life . . . Man's altruism has to grow. It is not enough for him to stand and deplore. That is less to mend things than to run from them. A positive charity is wanted; negation is not enough. In effect it needs a self-growth, which shall open out a finer self. It requires to absorb in 'feeling' something of the world beyond the self and put it alongside the interests of the very self . . . A great gift—some might say divine—comes to the 'self' when perceiving certain suffering external to itself it so reacts to it that suffering becomes its own, and is shared even as a 'feeling' . . . Altruism as passion . . . nature's noblest product; the greatest contribution made by man to life.

SIR CHARLES SHERRINGTON OM FRS FRCP FRCS   1857–1952
English physiologist
Man on His Nature

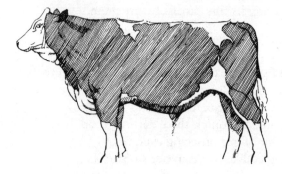

December 6

THE HARE, TO THE HUNTER

Are mindes of men, become so voyde of sense,
That they can joye to hurte a harmelesse thing?
A sillie beast, whiche cannot make defence?
A wretche? a worme that can not bite, nor sting?
If that be so, I thanke my Maker than,
For makying me, a Beast and not a Man.
. . . So that thou shewest thy vauntes to be not vayne,
That bragst of witte, above all other beasts,
And yet by me, thou neyther gettest gayne
Nor findest foode, to serve thy gluttens feasts:
Some sporte perhaps: yet Grevous is the glee
Which endes in Bloud, that lesson learne of me.

ANONYMOUS

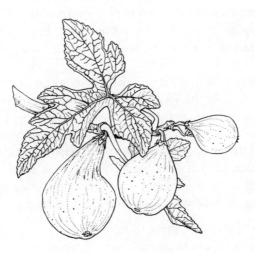

December 7

In the year 1774, being much indisposed both in mind and body, incapable of diverting myself either with company or books, and yet in a condition that made some diversion necessary, I was glad of anything that would engage my attention, without fatiguing it. The children of a neighbour of mine had a leveret given them for a plaything . . . understanding better how to tease the poor creature than to feed it . . . they readily consented that their father . . . should offer it to my acceptance . . . I undertook the care of three . . . Puss, Tiney and Bess. Notwithstanding the two feminine appellatures . . . they were all males.

. . . Puss grew presently familiar, would leap into my lap, raise himself upon his hinder feet, and bite the hair from my temples. He would suffer me to take him up, and to carry him about in my arms, and has more than once fallen asleep upon my knee. He was ill three days, during which time I nursed him, and by constant care, and trying him with a variety of herbs, restored him to perfect health. No creature could be more grateful than my patient after his recovery, a sentiment which he most significantly expressed by licking my hand, first the back of it, then the palm, then every finger separately, then between all the fingers . . . a ceremony which he never performed but once on a similar occasion . . . He would invite me to the garden by drumming upon my knee, and by the look of such expression, as it was not possible to misinterpret. If this rhetoric did not immediately succeed, he would take the skirt of my coat between his teeth, and pull it with all his force . . .

My intimate acquaintance with these specimens of the kind has taught me to hold the sportsman's amusement in abhorrence; he little knows what amiable creatures he persecutes, of what gratitude they are capable, how cheerful they are in their spirits, what enjoyment they have of life, and that, impressed as they seem with a peculiar dread of man, it is only because man gives them peculiar cause for it . . .

Bess died . . . young; Tiney lived to be nine years old, and . . . Puss is still living, and has just completed his tenth year . . .

WILLIAM COWPER 1731–1800
The Gentleman's Magazine May 28th 1784

December 8

[At the Guildford Market] I saw large rabbits picked up by the ears or scruff of the neck. The cages have very small openings and it is almost impossible to get animals in and out without hurting them and causing them panic.

MAGGIE NELMES
Compassion in World Farming December 1989

Although back-yard rabbits are often kept in very confined hutches, those in factory farms live in an entirely different world. It is a world in which exploitation for profit discovers new depths.

Unlike other livestock, rabbits cannot be reared under traditional 'humane' conditions. Because of high feed and labour costs, it is necessary to keep the does in a constant state of reproduction and to rear the progeny intensively in wire cages on wire floors . . .

One man can be put in charge of 450 does. Does often develop sore hocks from the wire floors and as a result of their distress, abort their litters . . .

Intensively reared rabbits are fed intensively—like battery chickens . . . no hay and greenstuffs . . . There are no specific guidelines for the transportation of rabbits in the UK . . . there is no recognized method for the slaughter of rabbits.

Agscene February/March 1985

There are companies who rear rabbits for butchers and who also sell rabbits to researchers.

Slaughter and torture : profit and gain,
Slaughter and torture : death and pain.

REBECCA HALL

December 9

When I was in my late thirties, a friend leaving for Europe left her cat with me—my first companion animal. I soon began to feel uncomfortable cuddling one animal while sticking a knife and fork into others. But change often takes time, it was a slow process until I stopped eating meat altogether. It's been said that if we had to kill the animals we eat, the number of vegetarians would rise dramatically and rapidly. But most people don't see, feel, hear the suffering of animals for dinner. It's not a question of saints vs sinners, but rather a society which brands animals as edibles and that's the pattern we're breaking. It's something each of us can do; it doesn't preclude other activities, and has no downsides. With a non-violent lifestyle, we save animals directly, and encourage discussion: which would you prefer, a stroll through a slaughter-house or an apple orchard?

HENRY SPIRA 1927–

American Animal Rights Coalition coordinator; former teacher and Civil Rights campaigner in the 1960s American South
Statement for this book

December 10

I have heard of several cows which have gone to enormous lengths to be reunited with their offspring. One old marshman in Norfolk told me of the time he had lived upriver from us and had sold a calf to another farmer. By road, the buyer's farm was about six miles away, but as the crow flies, it was just across the river.
The river was wider than the Dee, about eighteen feet deep in places and with strong tidal currents. From her field on one side of the river, the cow heard her calf calling to her from the other side. She broke through the fence, ran down to the river's edge and plunged straight in. Despite being swept downstream with the current, she managed to make it to the opposite bank and pulled herself out. From there she plodded back upstream and eventually found her way to the calf— much to the amazement of the new owner.

SUE WATTS
Farm Journal (Aberdeen) 17 November 1990

December 11

The huge man is still after me.
The man in the blood-stained apron.
The man who waved his long, sharp knife in the air,
Smiling at me.
The crowd urged him on, braying, 'kill! kill!'
And I saw the man's decaying teeth.
I saw all of this with my innocent, bulging eyes.
I saw fear and I saw death.
The huge man is still with me.
The man who smiled when the blood fountained onto my hot face.
I didn't want to look at the soil as the crowd gathered tighter.
Another man said a prayer in Arabic, with his hand stretched out
        towards the huge man.
Then I saw the huge man hand him the severed head of a sacri-
        ficed sheep;
A head looking at me with it's innocent, bulging eyes.
I was its last picture of life.
And I saw that my heart wasn't with the worshipping crowd.
For I knew when they started with the sheep they would end with me.
The whole world turned dark.
The huge man is still inside me.
The crowd is after me.
And I don't want to be eaten.

IRAJ JANNATIE ATAIE 1947–
Exiled Iranian poet and playwright

December 12

To adopt a true vegetarian diet is to join the process of healing the world. The gnosis of every great religion—so often subsequently betrayed and materialized—taught the compassionate life where killing has no part.

Far from being a deprivation, the herbivorous diet brings a life more abundant; better health, more strength, a clearer mind, a heart finding peace, knowing it has stolen nothing from its friends.

The needless murder of any living creature rests as a leaden cloud over the world, blotting out the joy of the sunlight.

The seemingly endless trail of suffering and hurt stretching behind us and the sea of blood which surrounds us, has brought a tragic forgetting. But evil was no part of the Creator's plan. We once knew an Eden and shall know it again.

There is no place for condemnation or disdain for those who have not yet taken the compassionate road, for all aggression in its myriad forms is a suffering which needs to be healed.

The true vegetarian looks with new, brighter and clearer eyes, learns a communion with Nature, a respect and an awe for its beauty and abundance and will seek ways to protect it from the ravages of the circle of poison which is killing the land and which, emanating from insecurity and greed shall, as surely as a circle is round, bring back disease and death, creation of man's unhealthy, unbalanced thoughts and desires, as yet hardly recognized.

The true vegetarian is a visionary, a pragmatist and a friend of Life.

REBECCA HALL

December 13

Humankind consumes around 140 million tonnes of meat a year—about 30 kilograms per person. The average in the USA is 111 kilograms per capita, in the UK, 68, in India, 1 kilogram. 90% of the meat in the USA is produced by cruel, unhygienic factory farming methods as is 90% of the chicken in the UK, and 55% of pigmeat.

The ranching of cattle in the world's rainforests is especially destructive. Each beefburger costs 55 square feet of rainforest to produce—that is half a tonne in weight of birds, trees and saplings.

Meat producers are spending vast amounts of money telling us how much we need it. They are worried, because medical evidence is telling us we don't need it. The National Advisory Committee on Nutrition Education UK states that meat is not only unnecessary in a healthy diet, but a hazardous extra.

Information from *New Internationalist* No. 215 Jan 1991

December 14

About ten years ago my son persuaded my wife and me to become vegetarians.
We were ready to receive his advice as both of us disliked the cruelty associated with the slaughter of animals and neither of us were very fond of meat.
He also argued that if the peoples of the world ate the grain instead of feeding it to the animals, and then killing them, there would be enough food for everyone.
These arguments, taken together, were enough to convert us and we have eaten no meat ever since.
What we did not realize was what pleasure we would discover when we moved over to this new diet.
Nothing in the world would persuade us to go back now, and most vegetarians would feel the same.

RT HON TONY BENN PC MP 1925–
British parliamentarian and author
A statement written for this book

December 15

Let no one regard as light the burden of his responsibility. While so much ill treatment of animals goes on, while the moans of thirsty animals in railway trucks go unheard, while so much brutality prevails in our slaughterhouses, while animals have to suffer in our kitchens painful death from unskilled hands, while animals have to endure intolerable treatment from heartless men . . . we all bear guilt for this.

ALBERT SCHWEITZER   1875–1965

❧ ❧

December 16

We confess before our Creator that as long as brutality and profit are allowed to direct the activities and existence of farm animals in America, we will all bear guilt for it.

Yet, we are determined that with sound thinking and spiritual presence, we shall all someday feel that burden of guilt lifted.

For make no mistake, the time will come when the ill-treatment of animals will end, the moans of thirsty animals in railway trucks will be only a painful echoing memory, and the suffering in slaughterhouses and kitchens will subside.

We shall endure until it does.
We shall speak and work
to make such a dream a reality.

REV DR MARC A WESSELS   1954–
Activist author, editor and lecturer
Message delivered at a Farm Animal Reform Movement rally in Washington DC on October 2nd 1989

December 17

The moral evils of a flesh diet are not less marked than are the physical ills. Flesh food is injurious to health, and whatever affects the body has a corresponding effect on the mind and the soul. Think of the cruelty to animals that meat-eating involves and its effect on those who inflict and on those who behold it. How it destroys the tenderness with which we should regard these creatures of God.

The intelligence displayed by many dumb animals approaches so closely to human intelligence that it is a mystery. The animals see and hear and love and fear and suffer. They use their organs more faithfully than many human beings use theirs. They manifest sympathy and tenderness towards their companions in suffering. Many animals show an affection for those who have charge of them, far superior to the affection shown by some of the human race. They form great attachments for man which are not broken without great suffering to them.

SISTER ELLEN G WHITE
Ministry of Healing Seventh Day Adventist Church

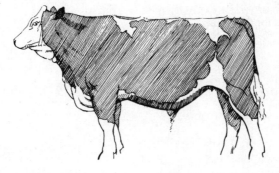

December 18

In 1989 when I was travelling across America to research grain monopolies for my book *Trading The Future*, some incredible facts came to light: over seventy per cent of the chickens in the factory plants—which were invented in the USA and now mop up ninety per cent of all American grain and soya bean—have salmonella (a bacterial disease). High dosages of antibiotics don't lower these levels; as one US Department of Agriculture official said, 'the only real solution is to quit eating the stuff [chicken].'

In the sixties and early seventies when huge soya and grain surpluses in the USA meant declining profits, the big grain traders persuaded the US government to give long-term interest-free loans to Second and Third World countries to set up their own intensive battery systems. These were dependent on US feedstuffs which were initially supplied under the US's international aid scheme (PL480). Having mopped up the surplus produce, price rises inevitably followed. So what seemed like a gift-horse to developing countries was suddenly a millstone around the neck as their borrowing increased to buy US feedstuffs for poultry which supplied a smaller and smaller section of their population with a 'luxury' protein.

The drug-disease-ridden chicken habit is like a double barb deep in the flesh of the recipient countries. While the minority eat the flesh of these wretched creatures, the majority go hungry. In times of shortage, scarce food supplies go to the chicken battery prisons which are more often than not given priority over the human population.

G F NEWMAN
Statement written for this book

December 19

From its humble beginnings of non-dairy vegetarianism, the vegan ethic has developed apace because there is no logical point where it can be stopped short of a new relationship with the rest of sentient creation. The purpose of the vegan movement was, and is, to meet head-on the religious heresy that animals were 'sent' for man's use. 'Sent' implies a sender—a view as unacceptable to the atheist as it should be blasphemous to the theist. It is the most evil concept ever to engage the mind of man. It drenches the world with the blood of innocent creatures; it distorts the natural order, and it leaves man with a burden of guilt which points directly to much of his own adversity. We suffer as a race because collectively we deserve no better.

DONALD WATSON 1910–
Founder and first Secretary of The Vegan Society, 1944; first person to use the term 'vegan'
The Vegan Winter 1989

December 20

For even unto this day, though the ages of ages have come and gone, these children of this earth are as much animal in their desires and habits, as they were when they were in the lower kingdoms.

If one should say that such a picture is untrue, let him first make clean his own heart and life, and then look out upon the Nations to witness how they live. If one should say that the picture is untrue, both as regards the Shambles and the Vice, let him purify himself in his own heart, and then ask himself the meaning of all the horrible exhibitions of passion with which he may meet at any hour and almost anywhere, how these dreadful things came to share so largely in the life of man. And if he would have a combined picture of him who became the world's Sin-offering, then let him lift up his heart unto the Hills of the Lord—Hills whose atmosphere is beautiful in purity—and then cast down his gaze on to the planes of the Earth, just when the hollow mockery of the Divine Love is most celebrated at Christmas, and he will behold a world whose paths run with blood, whose children live on the dead creatures slain on the altars of their passion for the flesh . . . And whilst the hollow mockery of rejoicing in the Divine proceeds within the Sanctuary, the Flesh of those Creatures slain upon the altars, awaits them in their homes.

REV JOHN TODD FERRIER 1855–1943
Herald of the Cross Vol III 1907

☙ ☞

December 21

On one occasion when a number of birds had been waiting for a long time on the shackles and were flapping their wings violently, three of the pluckers surrounded one turkey, placed their mouths close to its head and began to sing and shout loudly in the bird's face in accompaniment to a record on the radio 'So here it is, merry Christmas, everybody's having fun'. This caused more panic to the bird and much laughter among the pluckers.

Special Investigation for Compassion in World Farming
Report: *Agscene* Spring 1990

December 22

On Christmas Eve, our investigator who had spent three terrible days working in the slaughterhouse attached to the 'traditional farm fresh' turkey farm, decided he must at least purchase two of the birds and give them a good home. He purchased almost the last two live birds, a female whom he called Eve (as it was Christmas Eve) and a male called Adam.

These went to a temporary home in Hampshire. Our investigator's friend reported that Eve, who was badly maimed from her life in the intensive unit, spent most of the time inside the shed, whereas Adam loved to wander round the yard. When feeding time came and food was scattered on the ground, Adam would not eat. First he would go the shed and collect Eve and bring her out to the food. He would then take a beakful of food and place it on the ground in front of her.

And some people think that turkeys are unintelligent and insensitive.

Adam and Eve were taken to Wales where they will now spend the rest of their lives in spacious and very free-range surroundings.

JOYCE D'SILVA
Agscene Number 98 Spring 1990

December 23

'Do not ask me such deep questions just now, for I cannot see clearly, and it hurts me to look. The atmosphere is thick with the blood shed for the season's festivities. The Astral Belt is everywhere dense with blood. My Genius says that if we were in some country where the conditions of life are purer, we could live in constant communication with the spiritual world. For the earth here whirls round as in a cloud of blood like red fire. He says distinctly and emphatically that the salvation of the world is impossible while people nourish themselves on blood. The whole globe is one vast charnel-house. The magnetism is intercepted. The blood strengthens the bonds between the Astrals and the Earth . . . This time, which ought to be the best for Spiritual Communications, is the worst, on account of the horrid mode of living. Pray wake me up! I cannot bear looking; for I see the blood and hear the cries of the poor slaughtered creatures.'

ANNA BONUS KINGSFORD   1846–1888
From *Her Life, Letters, Diary and Work* by her collaborator Edward Maitland
George Redway London 1986

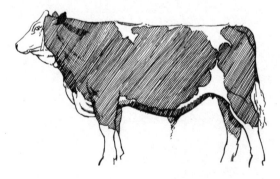

December 24

THE KILLIN' O' THE SOO

Near Christmas, an' the big fat soo
Grunts at her troch—I'll hae tae fill it,
She'll ne' guts mickle mair for noo
The fairmer says it's time tae kill it.

Oot cam ther flesher frae the toon,
Shairpened his aixe (I'm no' for seein')—
Her shrieks afore she wis brocht doo!
I hear them yet. The bluid wis fleein'.

Deid i' the glaur. The stye is toom.
(Whit had I done her pain tae lessen?)
Tremblin' I fled up tae ma room—
Disjasket, fleggit, scunnert, pechin'.

Sin that day I hae ne'er preed pork,
Nor flesh, nor fowl, nor even fishes . . .
That tasty morsel on yer fork
Wis killed. Tak vegetarian dishes!

JAMIE A SMITH
(So far as is known, this is the only poem ever composed in the Scottish
vernacular advocating vegetarianism)

December 25

The life of that one in whom the Christ-child is born must be a friend of the creatures. It could not be otherwise. The ox in the stall, the ass in the stable, the sheep in the byre, the dove in its cote, and all creatures in their several degrees of unfoldment, are related to such a life by indissoluble ties, even that of *the Oneness of all true life*, and by the fact that the gentle creatures have been the venues through which the soul has passed upwards in its true evolution before the Divine love. To be born in the stable or byre, and cradled in a manger, therefore, means very much more than to be born amid lowly conditions. For the soul truly was cradled amongst creatures. And when the Christ-child is about to be born within the Soul, the life awakens to the consciousness of its relationship to all the creatures, its duty unto them, and the service it must perform in making manifest the Divine Love then awakening within the Soul.

Of course all this implies the redeemed Life for the individual. It presupposes a very genuine sympathy with all the creatures, a sympathy so rich and full in manifestation that it could not hurt the creatures for its own pleasure nor cause them to be wounded, afflicted and killed on any pretext whatsoever . . . Unto such men and women the Abattoirs will be as hells in all their conditions.

REV JOHN TODD FERRIER 1855–1943
The Master, His Life and Teachings
The Order of the Cross

December 26

BECAUSE we as Unitarian Universalists affirm justice and respect for the interdependent web of all existence:

BECAUSE of our concern for the waste of resources associated with animal husbandry, knowing that twenty people can be nourished with the grains needed to produce enough meat for one person;

BECAUSE one third of the world's population goes to bed hungry, and 40,000 children each day die of starvation;

BECAUSE the United States has descended to seventeenth place in world health, and each year 1.6 million americans die from heart disease, stroke, cancer and other chronic illnesses that have been linked conclusively with animal fat and meat consumption, even many of our children now are suffering from fat-lined arteries (as shown by autopsies of motor accident victims) and 1,000 children had strokes in 1989;

BECAUSE the antibiotics, pesticides and other chemicals in animal feed enter into human diet, increasing our susceptibility to disease, allergies and immune system disorders; and

WHEREAS since 1960 about half the tropical rainforests in Central America alone have been destroyed to provide cheap pasture for the cattle that supply cheap export beef for American hamburgers, one 4oz hamburger representing the destruction of fifty-five square feet of rainforest;

WHEREAS uncounted species of irreplaceable plants and animals disappear as a result of the beef culture; WHEREAS more than half of the US lands are used for grazing, 307 million acres are in various stages of desertification; WHEREAS meat production requires from forty-five to one hundred times the volume of water and grain production;

WHEREAS thirty-five federal agencies and health organizations confirm that everyone over two years old should follow a diet much lower in fat and cholesterol;

THEREFORE BE IT RESOLVED that members of the Unitarian Universalist Association reduce their consumption of meat and other edible animal products and study means to conserve our precious agricultural resources to both save our environment and ensure adequate nutrition for all the 5.2 billion people on the planet.

General Resolution put forth by the Unitarian Universalists for the Ethical Treatment of Animals (USA)

December 27

To me being a vegan forms part of a boycott of the products of animal abuse in the hope that the abusers will eventually be forced out of business due to a reduction in demand. It is not a religion or a question of being *holier than thou* but a desire not to give economic support to the persecutors of animals. The exploitation of animals so pervades society that it is impossible to totally avoid its products, but it is very important that we do our very best. And it is also important to eat a *healthy* vegan diet, to take adequate exercise and to avoid harmful practices such as smoking so that our well-being will encourage others to go vegan too.

RONNIE LEE 1951–

Animal Liberationist given a ten year sentence in 1985 on a conspiracy charge for his animal rights activities.

A statement written from prison

December 28

. . . May our very indignation at the shocking sufferings inflicted wilfully on animals point out to us the pathway to the kingdom of pity toward all that lives, the Paradise once lost and now to be regained with consciousness?

When first it dawned on human wisdom that the same thing breathed in animals as in mankind, it appeared too late to avert the curse which, ranging ourselves with the beasts of prey, we seemed to have called down upon us through the taste of animal food: disease and misery of every kind, to which we did not see mere vegetable-eating man exposed. The insight thus obtained led further to the consciousness of a deep-seated guilt in our earthly being; it moved those fully seized therewith to turn aside from all that stirs the passions, through total abstinence from animal food. To these wise men the mystery of the world unveiled itself as a restless tearing into pieces to be restored to restful unity by nothing save compassion. The wise man could but recognize that the reasonable being gains his highest happiness through free-willed suffering . . . whereas the beast but looks on pain, so absolute and useless to it, with dread and agonized rebellion. *But still more to be deplored that wise man deemed the human being who consciously could torture animals and turn a deaf ear to their pain, for he knew that such a one was infinitely farther from redemption than the wild beast itself, which should rank in comparison as sinless as a saint.*

Races driven to rawer climates, and hence compelled to guard their life by animal food, preserved till quite late times a feeling that the beasts did not belong to them, but to a deity; they knew themselves guilty of a crime with every beast they slew or slaughtered, and had to expiate it to the god; they offered up the beast; and thanked the god by giving him the fairest portions of the spoil . . .

Legends have told us how wild beasts allied themselves in friendship with holy men—perchance not merely for the shelter thus ensured, but also driven by a *possible first gleam* of deep instinctive sympathy.

RICHARD WAGNER 1813–1883
Religion and Art: Essays

December 29

Massachusetts restaurant owner Bill Massey served up a menu including roast lion, fried alligator, loin of buffalo, wild boar and marinated hippopotamus to 106 'enthusiastic' diners. Massey drooled, 'It was absolutely delicious, the lion was fabulous. I marinated it in wine, oil and spices for thirty hours and roasted it to medium rare. It was tender, very lean and definitely the favourite among the diners.' Massey later expressed his respect for the animal kingdom: 'They are just slabs of meat like any other.'

Turning Point Magazine Number 11, July–September 1988 (England)

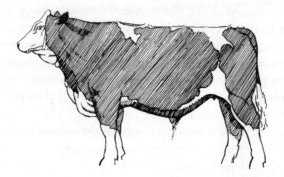

December 30

The habit of eating flesh has not only contributed to the physical, mental and moral degeneracy and degradation and affliction of the body, mind and heart of the people, but . . . the persistent habit for ages of nourishing the body upon flesh has so blinded the inner Vision of the Soul that the beautiful meanings of the Religion professed by the Western World have all been lost unto it; that the present awful Spiritual darkness even within the Church itself and its various Schools of Religious Thought, was due largely to the darkening effect upon the higher mind (or that which should reflect Spiritual and Divine things) of the long prevalence of the terrible evil.

But the day has surely dawned when a new and more beautiful vision of what life should be, has arisen before the mind of the Western World through many of its noblest sons and daughters beholding the awful evil which has imposed itself upon them for long ages. They have seen something of the fearful meaning attached to 'flesh-eating' and have put the evil thing away from them . . .

But what a commentary such an awakening is upon the professedly Christian Civilization which claims to be the highest ever reached! . . . What a commentary upon the nature and meaning of the Life of Christ, of His boundless Compassion and unfailing Pity! . . . What a commentary upon the vision of God in his beautiful nature, His unspeakable Purity and love, that his Holy Name should be associated with the institution of Flesh-eating; that He should be charged with making His children degrade themselves even to the level of the carnivorous animals which prey upon those less able to defend themselves, and of instituting the fearful abattoirs where creatures are made to lay down their lives to furnish flesh for Human Children; and that the shame of the shambles where the mutilated forms of the poor creatures are exposed to the view of every passer-by should be attributed to Him!

REV JOHN TODD FERRIER
Herald of the Cross Volume IV Part I

December 31

Sadly, on the morning of April 27th, Boyo (the magnificent turkey who featured on our postcards) was found dead. He had seemed on excellent form the previous day, so we believe he suffered a heart attack, due to his appalling built-in obesity . . . He took his role as guardian of the poultry run very seriously, his gobble resounding impressively around this little valley. 'Majestic' was the word that sprang to mind when he fluffed out his feathers to impress onlookers (which he never failed to do). However, Boyo was a travesty of what a turkey should be. In their wild state, turkeys can fly at fifty miles per hour, yet Boyo was only able to plod along at a snail's pace, barely able to lift his feet off the ground. Before burying him, we weighed him and he registered fifty pounds—around three and a half stones. Horrifically, many male breeding turkeys are even heavier, reaching the sixty-five pound mark (and remember the obscene 'Heavy Turkey' competition, when the 1989 winner tipped the scales at eighty-five pounds fourteen ounces). Presumably this is because breeders are selected for their huge size (Boyo was perhaps something of a runt). Yet these birds are slaughtered by a combination of electric shock (which may or may not be successful) and neck cutting, while hung upside down in painfully constricting shackles. They may, by law, be suspended for up to six minutes (and who can doubt it's sometimes longer?). Imagine the strain on their legs and hip joints (frequently diseased in these older birds) and the scene becomes intolerable. Imagine too the stress, pain and indignity of the artificial insemination procedures, upon which the modern turkey industry is totally reliant. Turkeys are highly sensitive to shocks of any kind.When Boyo died, the two females huddled up together in a state of apparent panic for some hours . . . All in all, the turkey industry of the 1990s is a disgrace in a supposedly civilized society. Yet to the general public turkey meat is still a clean, white, sanitized product, with a 'bootiful' image . . .

Boyo is now buried near the poultry orchard. We intend to plant a tree (something majestic—perhaps a chestnut or oak) in his memory. We had him a year, and have gained much from knowing him . . . In welfare terms, Boyo's life has, we believe, been of great significance. The Valley seems quiet now . . .

VIOLET SPALDING, CLARE DRUCE, IRENE WILLIAMS
Campaigners for farm animals
Chicken's Lib Newsletter Number 29

Epilogue

It often happens that the universal belief of one age, a belief from which no one was free nor could be free without an extraordinary effort of genius or courage, becomes to a subsequent age, so palpable an absurdity that the only difficulty is, to imagine how such an idea could ever have appeared credible.

JOHN STUART MILL 1806–1873
English philosopher and economist

The tender and humane passion in the human heart is too precious a quality to allow it to be hardened or effaced by practices such as we so often indulge in.

RALPH WALDO TRINE
Every Living Creature 1899

Animals are the defeated troops of a kingdom on the verge of annihilation, the scattered survivors with whom we ought finally to make peace.

GIANFRANCO AMENDOLA
Member of the Italian *Animalisti* party.
1992

Select Bibliography

Avyaktananda, Swami *The Liberation of Animals* (1970) Vedanta Movement, Bath UK

Arnold, Sir Edwin *The Light of Asia* (1884) Trübner UK

Bach, Dr Edward *Heal Thyself* (1931) C W Daniel UK (continuously reprinted)

Bryant, John *Fettered Kingdoms* J M Bryant UK

Bircher Benner, Dr *The Prevention of Incurable Disease* (1981) James Clarke UK

Cox, Peter *Why You Don't Need Meat* (1993) Bloomsbury UK

Dowding, Muriel *Beauty—Not The Beast* (1980) Neville Spearman UK

Ferrier, Rev John Todd *On Behalf of the Creatures* (1926) Herald of the Cross, Vol I, 1911; Vol II, 1906; Vol IV, 1908; Vol VII, 1911; Vol XII, 1938; *The Master, His Life & Teachings* (1913) The Order of the Cross, London UK (continuously reprinted)

Gupta, Surinda Nath *Vegetarianism: A Human Imperative* (1986) Bharatiya Vidya Bhavan, Bombay, India

Gompertz, Lewis *Moral Enquiries On the Situation of Man & Brutes* (18th century) (1992) Centaur Press UK

Hall, Rebecca *Voiceless Victims* (1984) Wildwood House (1993) PKP; *Animals are Equal* (1980) Wildwood House (1988) Rider (1993) PKP UK

Holmes-Gore, Rev V A *These We Have Not Loved* (1942) C W Daniel, Rennaissant Press (Order of the Cross); *Christ or Paul?* (1946 & 1989) Renaissant Press UK

Kapleau, Roshi Philip *A Buddhist Case for Vegetarianism* (1983) Rider UK

Kingsford, Dr Anna *Addresses & Essays on Vegetarianism* (1912) Watkins UK

Kloss, Jethro *Back to Eden* (1992) Jethro Kloss Family USA

Lascelles, Dr A *Pilgrimage With The Animals* Ed. Stanley King (1982) Seekers Trust UK

Mason, Peggy & Ron Laing *Sai Baba, The Embodiment of Love*. Gateway Books UK

Masri, Al-Hafiz BA *Islamic Concern for Animals* (1978) Athene Trust UK

Maitland, Edward MA *Life of Anna Kingsford* (1896) George Redway, London UK

Mason, Jim & Peter Singer *Animal Factories* (1980) Crown NY, USA

Moran, Victoria *Compassion The Ultimate Ethic* (1985) Thorsons UK

Ouseley, Rev G J R *The Gospel of the Holy Twelve* (1905) Christian Gospel Trust UK (reprinted)

Peters, Barbara Lynn *Dogs & Cats Go Vegetarian* (1988) Harbingers of a New Age USA

Porphyry *On Abstinence From Animal Food* (1965) Centaur UK

Pick, Philip (ed) *Tree of Life* (1977) A S Barnes NJ, USA

Rosen, Steven *Food For The Spirit* (1987 and 1990) Bala Books NY, USA

Robbins, John *Diet For A New America* (1987) Stillpoint USA

Regan, Prof Tom *The Case For Animal Rights* (1984) Routledge UK

Scharffenberg, John A MD *Problems With Meat* (1989) Woodbridge Press USA

Salt, Henry *The Humanities of Diet* (1897) The Humanitarian League

Szekely, Edmund Bordeaux (trans) *The Gospel of the Essenes* (1976); & Purcell Weaver *The Gospel of Peace of Jesus Christ* (1937) C W Daniel UK

Singer, Prof Peter *Animal Liberation* Random House NY, USA (1975) & Jonathan Cape UK (1990)

Spiegel, Marjorie *The Dreaded Comparison* (1988) Heretic Books UK

Sweeney, Noel LLB *Animals, Cruelty & The Law* (1990) Alibi UK

Thomas, Keith *Man & the Natural World—Changing Attitudes in England 1500-1800* (1983) Allen Lane; (1984) Penguin UK

Trine, Ralph Waldo *In Tune With the Infinite* (1897) Macmillan UK (1986); *Every Living Creature* (1899) Thomas Y Crowell USA

Wynne-Tyson, Esmé *The Philosophy of Compassion* (1962) Centaur UK

Wynne-Tyson, Jon *Food For a Future* (1988) Thorsons UK

Williams, Heathcote *Falling For A Dolphin* (1988); *Whale Nation* (1989) Cape UK

Yates, Geoffrey *Food, Need, Greed & Myopia* (1986) Earthright UK

Yntena, Sharon *Vegetarian Children* (1989) Thorsons UK

Index